Keeping It Fresh

A Love that Keeps On Growing

by

Peter and Beverly Caruso

Abba Ministries / Hands to Help Publishing

Keeping it Fresh - A Love that Keeps on Growing

by Peter and Beverly Caruso

ISBN 978-9629038-7-86

Unless otherwise indicated, scriptures are taken from
THE HOLY BIBLE, NEW INTERNATIONAL VERSION®.
NIV®. Copyright© 1973, 1978, 1984 by International Bible
Society. Used by permission of Zondervan. All rights
reserved.

Other translations include:
AMPLIFIED BIBLE © 1965 Zondervan. Used by Permission
CONTEMPORARY ENGLISH VERSION © 1995 American
Bible Society. Used by Permission
ENGLISH STANDARD VERSION © 2001 Crossway Bibles,
Used by Permission.
KING JAMES BIBLE Public Domain
NEW AMERICAN STANDARD BIBLE © 1995 Lockman
Foundation. Used by Permission
NEW LIVING TRANSLATION © 1996 Tyndale. Used by
Permission
THE MESSAGE © 1993 NavPress Publishing Group. Used by
Permission

Printed in the United States of America

Acknowledgments and Dedication

Many individuals have contributed to us as individuals and as a couple. The generations before us served as role models.

Our siblings, peers and children have encouraged and prayed for us.

Fellow ministers and laymen alike have spoken words of instruction, truth, correction and exhortation, helping us to understand our roles as man and woman, husband and wife.

To each of these we are indebted. Thank you, all.

Above all we are grateful to our Lord Jesus—our perfect Bridegroom—Who, through His sacrifice, has modeled unconditional love and acceptance, as well as perfect submission. We can only strive to live up to His example.

To Him, only, be the glory and honor.

Table of Contents

A Love That Keeps on Growing

You had not yet told me what *you* experienced in your little '50 Ford a few nights before. Now, only our second time together—and our first real date—you asked: "Will you be my special friend?" I had no idea what was behind that simple question.

I was not quite 18 and had violated my older brother's strong advice: "Never call a boy on the phone," he'd cautioned me. "If you do, you'll send a wrong message." But my phone call was not in order to flirt with you. I needed godly advice and sensed that you would give me some. You recently had spoken at our church's youth meeting and mentioned the affects of your parents' marriage problems on you as a boy. Now, with my parents' marital problems affecting me, maybe you could help me learn to cope.

So you picked me up from my job at Disneyland the next evening. We had a coke together and you drove me home. "Let's commit this to the Lord before you go in," you said. I was sitting on the Ford's bench seat, way over next to the door—you were behind the wheel. I began to pray. It was many months before you told me what happened next:

As you watched me pray you were thinking, *Hmm, she's cute, she's smart, she's spiritual. She's going to make some guy a good wife.* A bright light from nowhere filled the car and a voice, also from nowhere, said, "This is your wife."

The prayer time had barely begun, yet before I knew it you were reaching past me, opening the car door and saying, "I think you'd better go in now."

1

Keeping It Fresh

I thought, *What a strange guy. He says, "Let's pray," and then he practically pushes me out of the car.*

A week later, on our first date, you were asking me to be your *special friend.*

I think I've fulfilled that request. We've been best friends now for fifty years.

I love teasing that you didn't have any choice but to love me. **That** you have done well. Your love has been totally unconditional. It's been protective and supportive. Your love saw in a shy, obscure girl the potential that you nurtured me to fulfill. Your love has never wavered, never made me question your loyalty or fidelity.

Conversely, I was afraid to love; afraid I'd marry the wrong person and be miserable. I had to learn to love you. Yet loving you was easy and so natural. Before long I was asking the Lord if this love was the kind to base a marriage on.

You began talking about marriage right away, not blatantly, but subtly. I didn't know how to respond. Our prayer times at the end of each date proved to set the stage for the answer. One evening after Mom and Dad had gone to bed, we knelt side by side at the sofa in their family room. While we were praying God gave me a knowing: I knew that I knew that I knew that we were to be married. I'm so glad I waited until I knew. In fifty years I've never doubted for a moment that God meant us for one another.

What a life we've shared! Our wonderful children who all love our Lord. Now we get to watch not just grandkids, but our greats growing up. Thank you for being such a great Dad and Pappa to them.

I'm so blessed to have shared in your life's work. Being your wife as well as your ministry partner has been the greatest joy of my life. You've never held me back from developing my abilities. I've only received encouragement and… and a little embarrassment at you being my biggest—and most vocal—fan.

As we celebrate this half century mark I look back on all our past anniversaries: the first—a trip back to Disneyland, with me about to burst with the life of our first born. The 14th stands out as we rode in that pickup truck around the atoll of Majuro in the Marshall Islands so you could preach in Sam Sasser's church. On our 15th our congregation threw us a party and little Misty and David were the bride and groom in a mock wedding.

How many did we celebrate out on some camping trip with the kids? Then there was our 25th. Our kids threw a celebration a couple weeks early so that on *the day*, we could ride that ancient bus for 50 hours with a couple dozen other YWAMers on the way to a staff conference in Lindale, Texas. Number 34 was spent in Budapest, again with a group of YWAMers. On our 35th we were surprised by a houseful of friends and family—including emotional tributes from many we love. Number 40 was interrupted by Frank's death and we drove to Oregon to do his funeral. On our 46th I had been up all night in the hospital with Mom, and I wanted nothing more than to go to sleep—you kept me awake while I ate a Douglas Burger I didn't even want. But most anniversaries were shared over a lovely, restaurant meal for two, like the time at the Disneyland Hotel when the strolling musicians stopped at our table and sang for us *The Anniversary Song*.

So many memories! So much love.

3

Keeping It Fresh

I thought I loved you on our wedding day. I really knew nothing about love. Love is knowing that you'll come home to me. Love is laying my head on your shoulder, listening as you fall asleep and praying for God to use you for His purposes. Love is watching you play with— first our kids, then grandkids, and now the next generation yet.

Love is cooking a meal together, then you, without even being asked, helping me to clean it up. Love is analyzing our marriage together and sharing what we've learned with others so that maybe they will enjoy the kind of relationship we've found. Love is you sitting up all night on a train ride across Europe so that I can sleep the night away.

Love is having you interrupt my deskwork to ask me, "Have you stopped to eat lunch yet?" Love is hearing you come down the stairs in the morning—knowing that you'll wrap your arms around me and hold me for a long, lingering hug, then shower me with kisses.

Love is stopping—no matter what we're doing—to hug and share some kisses. Love is taking you a cold drink while you're pruning your trees that will give us fruit in the summer. Love is holding drywall tight to the ceiling while you nail it in place. Love is tucking up close to you and enjoying the fruit of our labor in the house we built together. Love is getting old together—and laughing at how we've gained weight, gotten stiff joints, and misunderstand what the other has said.

Love is exercising together so we won't get old. Love is something that is always growing. That's what we have—a love that just keeps on growing.

Your loving wife, Bev, September 5th, 2008

4

Chapter One

Is Marriage Obsolete?

The groom waited at the head of the aisle, beside him a row of handsome young men stood tall in tuxedo finery. The excited whispers of waiting family and friends hushed, then grew silent as the music signaled the beginning of the long awaited ceremony. We stood, and all eyes turned to catch a glimpse of the bride decked in white, waiting behind her lovely bridesmaids in their long summer gowns.

We didn't know the bridal couple. Our daughter would soon be marrying into this extended family and had been asked to be a bridesmaid. She winked as she passed us. Soon the minister started with those familiar old words, "Dearly beloved, we are gathered together today to join together this couple…"

I (Bev) settled into my seat filled with the emotion of the day. I love weddings; always have. "Do you take this woman…? Do you promise to love, honor and cherish her…?" Suddenly something wasn't right. *What did the minister just say? "…till love do you part?" I must have heard wrong. Surely that's not what he said.*

I was listening intently now. "Do you take this man to be your lawful wedded husband?" the minister asked the bride. "Do you promise to love, honor and cherish him till *love* do you part?"

I wasn't surprised when less than a year later that couple was processing a divorce. Clearly they had never intended for their marriage to last.

"Why bother getting married?"

Many young people are asking that today. With a divorce rate that continues to escalate, even among church-going families, the question bears examination. The news media and entertainment industry would have us believe a committed marriage is archaic, perhaps even becoming extinct. We might as well skip the vows. They'll be broken soon anyway. If there is to be a wedding, make it the best show possible. It's about making an impression, not about something sacred.

Some would have us believe, as one blogger wrote, that the majority of married men are "stuck in sexless marriages with nagging and bitching wives, but they choose not to divorce because they are afraid of being wiped out financially during divorce. Furthermore, the majority of relatively happy marriages are among very religious people, people choosing to live a simple lifestyle, people living in the rural South/Midwest, and recent Hispanic immigrants." This obviously bitter man went on to write, "If you are a normal American guy living in a large metropolitan area marrying a normal college-educated American woman who is looking for the American dream (a nice house, kids, good life), then you have over 95% chance of either getting divorced or trapped in a miserable marriage."[1]

---

[1] www.nomarriage.com

Is this to be believed? Of course you and I don't accept these statements. But is there truly no hope for marriage in the Twenty-First Century?

"A census report indicates that out of all currently married couples in the United States, only 5 percent had reached their fiftieth wedding anniversary. There are a number of reasons for this of course—chief among them the reality that the passage of years and the death of one or both partners will prevent many couples from reaching the half-century mark. Nevertheless, there's no denying that divorce in our society, along with other cultural developments designed to undermine the institution of traditional marriage, has resulted in fewer couples sticking it out for the long haul."[1]

Pete and I pastored two churches for a total of thirty-five years. We have been teaching marriage seminars since 1978—in various countries and cultures as well as here in the U.S. That's a lot of couples whose lives we've touched personally. We can avow that marriage *can* last. Marriage is not only alive and well, it is well worth whatever effort is required to keep it fresh. In fact, not only can it last, marital love can keep on growing!

Even as we watch the marriages of our children and now our grandchildren as well as many friends, we see that any man and woman who share God's view of marriage can have love that keeps on growing.

Sure it takes a lot of work—and commitment, selflessness, and stick-to-it-iveness. But it's so worth the effort. Why wouldn't it?! God designed marriage. He intended for marriage to bring satisfaction, fulfillment and completion to both the man and the woman.

---

[1] *Family News from Dr. James Dobson*, November, 2007.

Why do so many marriages lose their freshness?

Even among Christian couples? One reason is the problem of unreal expectations. Look at these common myths about marriage:

- There is such a thing as a *Happily-Ever-After-Marriage*.
- We both expect exactly the same things from marriage.
- Everything good in our relationship will get better.
- Everything bad in our lives will eventually disappear.
- My spouse will make me whole.

When we learn how God intended marriage to be and we align our thinking and expectations we can experience fullness of joy in our lives together. That's what this book is about. We're going to look into God's Marriage Manual. The Bible has much to say to help us discover His ways for marriage. We'll look at what God intended for husbands and wives and the ways He created us differently—and ways to accept those differences. Even celebrate them! We'll explore scientific findings, and sound statistical data. And we'll discuss communication styles, and techniques for discovering our talents and giftings. We'll examine God's wonderful gift to marriage—lovemaking. And of course we'll look at principles we personally have discovered during our fifty-year-long trek in the school of marital learning.

Whether your wedding is coming up next month, or your marriage is experiencing that seven year itch period, or perhaps, after thirty years together it has lost its luster, this book has plenty to offer to help you two experience a *love that keeps on growing.*

Chapter Two

Just a Contract - Or Is There More to It?

When a couple has a Christian marriage ceremony they are making covenant—a covenant before God and one another. There are nearly 300 references to *covenant* in the Holy Scriptures.

The Modern View of Marriage

Marriage today is viewed essentially as a contract—a bilateral agreement[2] between two parties totally dependent upon the performance of the agreement. Under a contract, if one party fails to perform according to the contract, the other party no longer is obligated to perform; he is no longer bound by the terms of the contract.

The Historical View of Marriage

Until recent years, the concept of marriage, even in society at large, and especially in the church, has been that of a covenant, not a contract.

---

[2] An obligation "having terms affecting both sides reciprocally arranged symmetrically on opposite sides of an axis." Webster's Old World College Dictionary, 2009.

We believe that this exchange of the value of covenant for the value of contract is responsible for a major portion of the abuse and dysfunction currently taking place in families. Let's examine it closely. The covenant value in marriage would have each marriage partner say to the other, "I am irrevocably committed to you until death separates us. My commitment to you has nothing to do with your performance or any choice you make. It is a unilateral commitment[3] before God unto death." This is the commitment that Jesus made to us when He said, *"I will never leave you or forsake you."*[4]

On the other hand, the contract value would say, "I'll keep my end of the bargain if you keep yours. If you make me unhappy or don't do what you promised, then I will leave you and find someone else who makes me happy and keeps his or her promises. And if you leave me, then I will definitely leave you and find someone else."

The biblical concept of marriage is that of a blood covenant, a concept which has been known and practiced for centuries in the east, but is little known nor understood in the west. The word means: agreement, contract, convention, treaty, promise, and pledge.

A blood covenant is the closest, most sacred, most enduring, binding agreement known to men. When the ancients made such a covenant, they made a commitment to each other more valuable than even their own lives. When entering into such a covenant, they made the basic commitment that "all I have and all I am is yours. Your enemies are my enemies, and I am ready to give up even my life for you, if need be."

---

[3] An obligation made by one individual," one-sided; relating to only one of two or more." Webster's Old World College Dictionary, 2009.
[4] Hebrews 13:5

Such a covenant was virtually never broken. It was such a sacred commitment that a man would die before he would dishonor himself by breaking a covenant.

The first biblical accounts of covenant were initiated by God with Abraham when he was still called Abram. The first was when God told Abram to bring "a heifer, a goat, and a ram, each three years old, along with a dove and a young pigeon." Abram cut each of the animals in half and God sent a blazing torch to pass between the pieces. On that day the Lord made a covenant with Abram and said, "To your descendants I give this land."[5] The second covenant between God and Abraham was expressed as circumcision of the foreskin of every male.[6]

Notice that both covenants had the shedding of blood. That is how God planned it for the wedding night when a virgin first gives herself to her husband. Her hymen[7] is broken, blood is shed and the vows they just exchanged a few hours earlier are sealed in a blood covenant. Of course we live in a fallen world so it's not always this way. Whether there is an intact hymen, or it has been broken by injury during sports activity, or by sin, God wants us to view marriage as a covenant.

It is astounding that Almighty God would make covenant with man, committing all He is and all He has to us mere mortals. Jesus took upon Himself the punishment for our breaking of that covenant when we sin. In His establishment of the New Covenant and shedding Christ's blood on the cross, God offered to all

---

[5] Genesis 15:18
[6] Genesis 17:11
[7] A hymen is a fold of mucous membrane partly closing the external orifice of the vagina in a virgin.

who will receive, an irrevocable,[8] indissoluble[9] covenant commitment.

To summarize: a covenant is a commitment made to another party in the presence of God and is independent of the performance of the other party. The concept of covenant—as in marriage—then, is a unilateral, irrevocable, in dissoluble commitment valid until death.

The marriage covenant is a lovely picture lived out by faulty humans, of that covenant which God has made with man. It is a beautiful thing when two individuals, who each are in a covenant relationship with God, choose to make a covenant in marriage. So when we marry, we are making a legal, binding agreement for life to forsake all others and commit our lives to walk together. We are choosing to turn away from any involvement with another and to keep ourselves for one another only. This is not only at the physical level, but includes any entanglement of emotions with another. By choosing to do this, we go against the norms of today's society. Yet in doing so, we lay a foundation for a life-long marriage—with no backdoor. A marriage for keeps.

Of course it is not humanly possible to fulfill such a covenant without the divine help of God. Only as both husband and wife draw upon His strength as we follow the biblical pattern of marriage, and as we fulfill the job descriptions laid out in the Scriptures for husband and wife, will we be able to keep this covenant.

Let's examine those biblical patterns and principles together which *we* discovered in *our* marriage, often

---

[8] That which "cannot be revoked, recalled, or undone; unalterable." Webster's Old World College Dictionary, 2009.
[9] "Not dissolvable; incapable of being dissolved or separated; incapable of separation; perpetually firm and binding; indissoluble; as, an in dissoluble bond of union." The Online Plain Text English Dictionary.

learned the hard way. They have blessed us in our fifty years together.

We have the privilege of reclaiming and enjoying this beautiful gift of God called marriage.

Is Marriage Obsolete?

Chapter Three

Where Is This Family Headed?

The family piles into their SUV and heads down the highway. All along the way there are interesting things to see. When something is especially interesting, we pull over and get out, sometimes at a scenic overlook, sometimes to get a double decker ice cream cone. After two or three hours we're ready to turn around and head for home. With no destination, there is no incentive to keep going.

Some marriages are like that. No plan, no goals. The couple simply lives from day to day. Children join the couple and together they stumble through life.

Let's examine the **Goals of a *Typical* Twenty-First Century Marriage**:

• Live together – Many couples are living together yet never become a family. As long as they are sexually attracted to one another and can get along reasonably well, and it is convenient, they will stay together.

• Pay the bills; make money – This seems to be the primary goal of most couples: live from day to day, strive to acquire things, try to keep up with the latest fads and fashions, or at least avoid bankruptcy.

- Look good – This seems to be the prime motivating factor for many in today's gotta-look-good-world. This includes our physical appearance—whether losing weight or building muscle, our wardrobe, the car we drive, the house we live in, and even the places where we eat and go for vacation. Our decisions are based more on what others will think than on than how we consciously choose to live.

- Have fun – If we analyze actions, we will come to the conclusion that we all seek happiness. For most of us, every act is in fact a search for happiness even if on the surface it doesn't appear so. Happiness is the main goal. Every day we're assaulted with reminders of ways we can enjoy life, find excitement, and have fun. Amusement parks, fancy cars, delicious food, unique experiences, and charming people are supposed to make us happy. Of course not all actions produce happiness. The motive may be happiness, but often the result doesn't bring the desired feelings. When we look closely at the lives of those who have all the time and money to pursue fun and happiness, we discover that often they are the most unhappy among us. Their divorce rate, their suicide rate, and their misery rate often exceeds that of normal, average working Justin and Jessica.

A number of years ago a group of couples met together weekly. The group spent several sessions talking about what we wanted for our families. We examined the Scriptures, we brainstormed, and we debated. Finally we decided each would use the next week to individually list our goals for our family.

When we came together again we assembled the following set of **Goals for a Christian Family**.
- To develop complete unity between husband and wife in thought, attitude, and purpose.

- To develop in the household an atmosphere of God's presence that would influence all who enter.
- To develop within the children a reverence for God, His Word, His church, and His service that would enable each to live for Him when independent of the home's direct influence.
- To develop relationships through which each member of the family could have all physical, emotional and mental needs met.
- To fully develop each family member's potential in life by mutually honoring and nurturing one another's unique role and ministry.
- To develop freedom from all types of bondage to earthly values, including being in debt.

Many years have passed since then. Most of those couples are now grandparents. Yet these goals have proven to be a strong foundation for any home.

In their *Family Living Seminars*, our daughter and son-in-law, Debbie and Dean Peterson, offer a working definition of a family that helps to clarify those goals:

"A family is a living laboratory where each member has the opportunity to practice the principles of Christian living in a setting where each member is accepted for who he or she is at the moment, forgiven for their failings, and nurtured and encouraged to become ever more like Christ."

It may seem strange to talk about family in a book on marriage. We've done this intentionally. The couple is the smallest family unit. When a couple gets married, they are a family. Even if no children are ever added, they are a family. If each couple would view our marriage that way, we could avoid some of the issues that can wreak havoc on our marriages.

Perhaps we can stop right now to determine the goals for our family. Perhaps they'll differ from those listed

17

years ago. Taking time to agree upon them, and writing them down, can be one of the best investments ever.

_____

_____

_____

_____

_____

_____

_____

_____

_____

_____

_____

_____

_____

_____

_____

Objectives

Once we know our goal as a couple–and a family— we can focus on our objectives. We could also call this our purpose. The age-old question stands:

What am I here for?

Functioning in a marriage and as a family provides, among other things, the setting for learning a wide range of lessons in life, and for practicing until we *get it right*. We each can learn to relate to one another, to control our person and our responses to situations. There is so much more we can learn in the context of the marriage and family.

Some families have a clear-cut purpose: The Giffords ride their tandem bicycle in bike-a-thons to raise money for Bibles in Rwanda; the Turnbulls love to help save marriages; the Schuerman family live in Eastern Europe to take the message of Christ to the lost; the Lukasses are in Brazil to care for orphans; Joel and Faith Winger have adopted seven children, some from the developing world, to shower them with love.

When our purpose is birthed in prayer, when that purpose is valued and shared by each family member—and kept at the forefront in all decision making—the family is drawn together and held together by that purpose. We can endure sacrifice and hardship when we know our goals and share our purposes. We might even choose to post them somewhere as a reminder to ourselves and to others.

Perhaps you'd like to write your family's purpose here.

_____

_____

_____

_____

_____

_____

_____

Keeping It Fresh

Chapter Four

God's Marriage Analogy

God is the greatest story teller of—all eternity. Throughout the centuries He gave us stories: of godly men and women; evil rulers and subjects; obedient families and rebellious tribes. God intended that we would learn from these accounts. His most beautiful story lesson is that of Christ and His bride, the Church. He gave us a living illustration of that love story in the form of marriage—by comparing the relationship between a man and woman with that of Christ and the Church. If only we will learn from it and enjoy marriage as He intended it to be!

We find the details spelled out in Chapter Five of Ephesians. It begins with verse 21 which so often is skipped over by teachers and preachers. After listing a series of admonitions: walk diligently; be wise; make good use of time; understand what the will of the Lord is; don't be drunkards; be filled with the Holy Spirit; be prepared to participate with others when gathering together; be thankful; He tells us we are to *submit ourselves one to another in the fear of God.* Regarding this passage, Matthew Henry wrote that there is "a mutual submission that Christians owe one to another, condescending to bear one another's burdens: not advancing themselves above others, nor domineering over one another and giving laws to one another."[1] This principle correlates with the many other passages of scripture we like to refer to as *The One Anothers,*[2] where we are told eleven times to *"love one another:"* in four passages the Apostle Paul instructs the Church to *"greet one another with a holy kiss:"* in three more verses he says that we should *"encourage one another:"* in another twenty verses we're given twenty-nine additional ways to express our love *to one another*.

Mutual Submission

Verse twenty-one of Ephesians Five makes it clear. We are to *"submit to one another."* I love that, not because it says Pete must submit to me, but because it says that all Christians are to be submissive to one another. Most who teach on the roles of husband and wife skip that verse and rush on to begin with the next verse.

Verse 22 says *"Wives, submit yourselves unto your own husbands, as unto the Lord."* Oh, how mistaken I was in my understanding of the meaning of that passage.

I accepted Christ at the age of six and grew up with a desire to please Him. I heard plenty of messages on wives submitting to their husbands. I thought I knew what it meant. My role model of a good wife was my Grandma Byrum. She and Grandpa had such a good relationship—the best! From what I could see, Grandma never argued with Grandpa. She never even disagreed with him. She met all his needs without complaint, even

---

[1] *Matthew Henry's Complete Commentary on the Whole Bible,* Matthew Henry, 1706-1721
[2] God Gift of *Friendship - Tools for Improving Relationships*, by Beverly Caruso, available from www.PeteandBevCaruso.com.

when inconvenient for her. And she was a happy and contented woman! I know; I asked her. I tried to be the kind of wife I saw in her.

Married Three Years and Never Had a Fight

My husband began bragging from the pulpits where he preached as a ministerial student that we had been married for three years and had never had a fight. Some of those host pastors told him he was a liar for making such a statement. He wasn't lying! I would sit there asking myself, *How can two have a fight when one never expresses a differing opinion?* I didn't point out to him that it was not to his credit that we had such a peaceful relationship.

Yet I was growing frustrated. I had completely merged myself into Pete: I no longer knew my own opinions. Finally in my longing for fulfillment I wondered, *What does the Bible really teach about the role of the wife?*

We had plenty of English translations of the Bible so I studied them all, researching every reference to wives, marriage and mothers.

So Just What Is Submission?

I began by examining the original Greek for an understanding of that awful word translated *submit*:

This word was a Greek military term meaning *"to arrange [troop divisions] in a military fashion under the command of a leader."* In non-military use, it was *"a voluntary attitude of giving in, cooperating, assuming responsibility, and carrying a burden.*

The Greek Lexicon defines it:
1. to arrange under, to subordinate
2. to be subject, to put in subjection
3. to subject one's self, to obey

23

4. to submit to one's control
5. to yield to one's admonition or advice
6. to obey, to be subject to

Discouraged, I plodded on in my search for understanding…

The Contemporary Version seemed a little softer, *"Wives should always put their husbands first, as the church puts Christ first."* [3]

Be Subject To

I couldn't get away from the phrase in the original: be subject to. Then I thought about those women who are married to alcoholics. They certainly are subject to the life of a wife of an alcoholic. He might come home smelly and sick. He might spend all their money on booze. He might even slap her around.

I married an Italian-American (an FBI as he likes to say: a **F**ull **B**looded **I**talian). He liked spicy food and tended to talk loud and be a little audacious. I was subject to the life he provided even though often I was embarrassed when he blurted out loudly, "Praise You, Jesus!" while pumping gas or, "Hallelujah!" while walking a supermarket aisle with me.

While I was on my quest for understanding I heard a pastor's widow compare submission to the process a person must go through to get a permit to build a building or even to add a room to a house. The plans must be carefully prepared and submitted, in the form of blueprints, [4] to the authorities, called the Building Department in most cities. On the agreed upon date the

---

[3] Ephesians 5:22, Contemporary Version
[4] A blueprint is a set of formal drawings (before modern technology it was printed on blue paper, or blue ink on white paper), that show the walls and windows, electrical, plumbing, etc. It also includes sketches of the exterior elevations, etc. and any necessary information for the officials as well as the builders.

contractor or homeowner returns to learn whether the plans have been approved or denied. Or he might be told to resubmit with necessary changes. In some cases the builder must submit several successive sets of modified plans. Sometimes, though not often, the plans are completely rejected.

I understood and liked this picture. Instead of merging her personality into her husband's, a wife is supposed to be a contributing partner in the marriage. Her ideas, opinions, fears, and dreams are to provide an important portion of the information her husband needs in order to make the final decision in a matter.

One added blessing this construction analogy provided me deals with the situations *when one's submission is rejected.* If the contractor doesn't like the answer he receives, he can go over the head of the person at the front desk to a higher authority. Sometimes I go over Pete's head and tell *Pete's higher authority* that I believe Pete's decision is going to lead us to disaster, or simply that I don't like the fact that he has rejected my idea. A few times God's response has been something like, "Leave it to me, he'll soon be right where I want him, flat on his face where he will learn what I want him to learn."

This understanding of submission was totally liberating to me. Of course, implementing it took adjustment, not only on my part but on Pete's as well. He was not used to having me express opposing perspectives.

Most women today, after two generations of Women's Lib, find the opposite problem when applying the principle of submission. Women are accustomed to readily offering their opinions, to freely expressing their wants and dreams. If they have lived away from their parents' home for long, they probably are accustomed to living their lives pretty much the *way* they want to, and *when* they want to. For them, offering all that they are—their dreams, wants, needs, fears, and opinions—available to any man, even their husband, does not come easily, even if they know the above principle.

I don't deny that some good has come from the Women's Lib Movement. On the whole, women are being paid more equitably. More women hold positions of leadership in most arenas of life. A woman is now free to pursue any career she chooses. One of the downsides is that the blurring of the roles has resulted in men not knowing how to act. We women have communicated, "I'm quite capable of taking care of myself, thank you." If a man expresses traditional deference to a woman in public, such as opening a door for her, he may receive a rebuff for not treating the woman as an equal. Men on the whole have been left emasculated. They've lost respect for themselves—as a gender and as individuals.

A Feminist Looks at Today's Marriages

Before we go on to hear from Pete about God's pattern for husbands, let's look at what lawyer-turned-freelance writer Charlotte Allen told a group of feminist-oriented college students.

"Traditional manners and extended families allowed women more freedom, privacy, power and self-worth than they gain from the fragmented families and communities produced by the modern 'cult of self-fulfillment.'

"Extended families have been the basic social unit worldwide and throughout history, even when people physically reside in nuclear households," Allen claimed citing several studies. "People in such families have important relationships with different family members, so that their self-worth and contentment do not depend on a lifelong emotional and intellectual romance with their spouses."

Allen described a way of life that is now largely abandoned. It was characterized by families bound by duty and necessity rather than by a quest for self-fulfillment. They were economically productive units in which women did socially respected work in or near the home, children helped with chores, and older people helped raise children.

"American women," she explained, "who moved to the suburbs after World War II found themselves isolated from any extended family or community. Their only long-term relationships were within the household, and they were forced into inescapable intimacy with only one person. Their husbands became their only source of adult conversation.

"Suddenly, women began noticing that men weren't 'supportive,' or 'responsive,' and didn't share their feelings. Their discontent focused on the only family relationships they had left.

"Middle-class women and young people began emphasizing 'self-fulfillment' and 'feelings.'" Allen explains, "and eventually every generation embraced the new value structure. Baby boomers retained the emotional desires of adolescents well into middle age. Older people gathered in their own communities and no longer had much influence on the young.

"Today's youth are the first generation to be raised within the 'cult of self-fulfillment' rather than being converted to it. They are a 'Me Generation' upon a 'Me Generation,' They are both frightened and frightening.

"Now we have no traditional customs because contact between the generations has withered," Allen continues. People "have to reinvent everything" for themselves.

Marriage, childbirth, child-raising and aging are wholly new and terrifying experiences, rather than basic, familiar phases of life.

"The postwar move from settled extended families and neighborhoods also put women's working lives and self-esteem in crisis. Women's work maintaining the household came to be seen as second-class drudgery, a mere support system for the breadwinner. They were not respected unless they had a career. By now, every woman is expected to be a 'Superwoman' who does it all, balancing a full career and a happy family." [5]

Most of us today are unaware of this slide from centuries of traditional family life to what is the norm today: Husbands and wives who are isolated from their nuclear families trying to single-handedly meet one another's needs and rear their children. Is it any wonder that few marriages last?

Did God Make a Mistake?

God knew what Twenty-First Century wives were going to face. He also knew that a two-headed creature is a monster. We once saw a two-headed snake in a zoo. If both heads had tried to go their own way, it would have rent the snake in two. One head had to take the leadership. A two-headed marriage is a terrible thing to behold—and worse to experience, for the couple and for their children.

In creating marriage, God gave us a beautiful picture of Christ and His church. He also created a setting where those of the following generations could be nurtured and trained into the individuals He intended them to become.

[5] In a lecture at the College of William & Mary on March 29, 1994, according to John Crouch, Attorney at Law, Arlington, Virginia. Copyright John Crouch 1994, on his web site: http://patriot.net/~crouch/atrj/allen.html

Our Ephesians passage goes on to describe the kind of husband Jesus is to the Church. By presenting this analogy, God, through the Apostle Paul, is teaching husbands how to love their wives. Pete takes over the narrative now so he can address the men directly.

Keeping It Fresh

Chapter Five

A Leader She'll Want to Follow

Just as learning her role as a wife was an on-going process for Bev, so I had much to discover about how to be a godly husband to my wife. And I'm still learning after over fifty years. Our key passage in Ephesians Chapter Five is quite lengthy, so let's take it phrase by phrase:

A Husband is a Head
"For the husband is the head of the wife, as [in the same way as] Christ also is the head of the church."[1] This is not presented here as theory, rather as a factual statement. Husband is an office—the Head of the Marriage. The woman we took as our wife is our first responsibility in life. For a few men this comes naturally. The rest of us must study and work at it.

A husband is therefore a priest; the church he pastors is his family. That makes us the priest of our family. *"Here is a trustworthy saying: If anyone sets his heart on being an overseer [a priest], he desires a noble task. The overseer must be above reproach, the husband of but one wife, temperate, self-controlled, respectable, hospitable, able to teach, not given to drunkenness, not*

---
[1] Ephesians 5:23

31

violent but gentle, not quarrelsome, not a lover of money. He must manage his own family well and see that his children obey him with proper respect. (If anyone does not know how to manage his own family, how can he take care of God's church?) "[2]

What Does it Mean to Be the Head?

First, some typical mistaken expressions of *headship*:

- Being a head does not mean being a **dictator**! A demanding, threatening, overbearing man who lords it over his wife and children, demanding his way, and requiring that they serve him.
- Being a head is not being a **spectator** or a **passive observer** who leaves the marriage and home responsibilities up to his wife. She may be better at handling the check book or scheduling household details, but he doesn't leave to her the emotional weight of those tasks. God never intended the woman to carry the responsibilities of the family by herself. God said of Abraham, *"For I have chosen him, so that he will direct his children and his household after him to keep the way of the Lord by doing what is right and just, so that the Lord will bring about for Abraham what he has promised him."* The Darby Translation starts with, *"For I know him that he will..."* [3] The Amplified Version says, *"For I have known (chosen, acknowledged) him [as My own]*[4]
- Being a head is not being **slothful**. Solomon wrote: *"If a man is lazy, the rafters sag; if his hands are idle, the house leaks."* [5]

---

[2] 1 Timothy 3:1-5
[3] Genesis 18:19
[4] Amplified
[5] Ecclesiastes 10:18

- Being the head of the home means being **an administrator**. Headship is an office and a function, not a status that makes one superior. As the head a man oversees the care and training of the children, their chores, discipline and homework, he is aware and involved in the finances, the family's social life, the upkeep of the house such as home repairs and maintenance. He doesn't necessarily do it all, and she may make arrangements for it to happen. But he sees to it that it gets done; he carries the emotional responsibility.

Love Your Wife

Guys, we need to understand that this is not a suggestion, it's a command. Paul goes on to instruct the man how to be the head, *"Love your wife."*[6] Many of the needs women share can be summed up in that one word *love*.

God answers *our* prayer, gives *us* possessions, and supplies all *our* needs because He loves us with Agape Love. Our response to Him is Phileo Love: Responsive Love. Our love for God is based on what is done to us or for us.

The history of this word *love* in Ephesians Five can help us here. The word in the original language of the Bible is *agape*. It means *giving one's self; self-sacrificing.* How much did Jesus give up for the church? 100%! He laid down His life for her. That's how much Christ loved the church—it was sacrificial love.

During the renaissance period when Shakespeare was writing his plays, he portrayed the knight in shining armor riding off to war. He turned to see his fair maiden at the castle door waving her handkerchief and he felt emotions within his breast. Emotions became a part of

---

[6] Ephesians 5:25

the word *love*. As years passed, Hollywood gradually added sex to the meaning. If we were to ask just about anyone on the street now, "What is *love*?" the answer usually would include the idea of sex.

When Jesus shed His blood on the cross He wasn't having an emotional experience, He wasn't having gushy feelings for us. He went to the cross because He loved us–with Agape Love. He knew that without Him giving His life, we would spend eternity in hell.

How, then, Are We to Love Our Wives?

Our love is to be *"as Christ loves the church"*[7] – Jesus gave Himself up for her. He gave His very life for her. Christ loves us because it is His nature to love. He doesn't love us based on anything we do or don't do. His love is an aggressive love—Agape Love.

Sanctify Her

The next verse says, *Jesus "gave Himself up for her that He might sanctify her."*[8] *[Emphasis mine]* When a man sanctifies his wife he sets her apart *for a special purpose.* Setting her apart means her husband is to love her in such a way that she can understand and receive his love.

A woman can feel her husband's love when he has an understanding attitude toward her. The impetuous disciple Peter wrote, *"Husband, live with your wife and understand her. Honor her as the weaker vessel. If you don't, you will find it impossible to pray."*[9] The *New American Standard Version* states Peter's instruction this way: *"Live with [her] in an understanding way, as with someone weaker, since she is a woman; and show*

---

[7] Ephesians 5:25
[8] IBID, verse 26
[9] 1 Peter 3:7

her honor as a fellow heir of the grace of life, so that your prayers will not be hindered.[10] As we'll see later, it is not that she is inferior, or a weakling. God is saying that she is one who should be valued and protected, out of love.

A man might ask: How can I live with her with understanding when she can't even understand herself?

- We can learn all we can about women's needs in general – those things that apply to most women.
- We can get to know our own wife's particular needs.

We can ask such questions as:

- Has moving away from your family and friends left you feeling alone?
- Has my job change, or you going back to work after having babies, caused emotional stress for you?
- Am I so involved in my work that I don't give you enough of my time?

We can also consider:

- Does she fear what could possibly happen to you?
- We can see to it that she has several hours at least once a week to do just what she wants to do.
- We can be mindful of how she stands with the Lord and encourage her spiritual growth.
- We can be aware of how we react to her during *that time of the month.*

Wash Her with Our Words

Jesus washes His church with His Words, *"that he might sanctify and cleanse it with the **washing of water by the word.**"*[11] *[Emphasis mine]*

---

[10] 1 Peter 3:7 New American Standard Version
[11] Ephesians 5:26

Keeping It Fresh

Conversation is an important need in any relationship, especially a marriage relationship. Jesus cleanses the church by the washing of the Word. As we read the Word and as we hear it preached, it washes us. The Word cleanses us. It comforts us. It encourages us. So Jesus sanctifies us. He sets us, His body, apart for special care. With His Word Jesus calmed the storm. He forgave sin. He brought peace to a troubled heart. He comforted the grieving. The Word does this for us. As a husband we can cause our wife to feel like a *nothing*, or we can produce a radiant, self-confident woman with our words.

How can we produce a radiant woman? Through praise! While one husband was criticizing his wife he called her a monster. She responded defensively, "You made me the monster that I am."

The Amplified Bible says, *"Let each one of us make it a practice to edify, to strengthen, and to build up his neighbor."*[12] If we are commanded to do this to our neighbor, how much more should we for our covenant wife?"

The world may look upon physical beauty, but God looks at the heart. So should we. *"Let us eagerly pursue the up-building of one another."*[13] We can tell our wife that we need her; that she meets our needs; that we value her opinions. We can tell others in front of her how wonderful she is. Our words should be life to our church: words of life, words of protection, words of forgiveness, words of security. Our words should wash away her fears—or they can wound, hurt, or even torment her.

By this time you may be thinking that the role of husband is nothing but sacrifice and giving out. Of

[12] Romans 15:2
[13] Romans 14:19

36

course we want to know: *What's in it for me?* In the next chapter we'll see some benefits of The Marriage Analogy of Christ and the Church, for both Christ and for a husband.

Keeping It Fresh

Chapter Six

What's In it for Me?

It is true that our role as a husband is full of self-sacrifice. If we only look at it that way, though, we're missing the point. Our Ephesians Five passage says that Jesus *"loved the church and gave Himself up for her that He might sanctify her, having cleansed her by the washing of water with the word [so]* **that He might present to Himself the church in all her glory, having no spot or wrinkle or any such thing; but that she should be holy and blameless.**" [1] *[Emphasis is mine.]* The Message Bible puts it this way: *"Husbands, go all out in your love for your wives, exactly as Christ did for the church—a love marked by giving, not getting. Christ's love makes the church whole. His words evoke her beauty. Everything he does and says is designed to bring the best out of her, dressing her in dazzling white silk, radiant with holiness. And that is how husbands ought to love their wives.* **They're really doing themselves a favor**—*since they're already "one" in marriage."* [2] *[Emphasis mine]*

---

[1] Ephesians 5:25-27
[2] Ephesians 5:25-28 The Message

Present Her Back to Yourself

"...that He might present [the church] to himself."[3]
Jesus continues to work on us. With words of
encouragement and exhortation He helps us to grow. He
intercedes for us to the Father. Why? In order to present
us—His church—back to Himself at the Marriage
Supper of the Lamb.[4] He's looking for a bride that is
beautiful. We, His bride, are being made that now, in
this life. As a husband we are in the process of making
our wife what she is. We shape her attitudes by what we
do and say as her head. *"The woman is the glory of the
man."*[5]

Take a look at these passages for a greater
understanding of God's view of this:

- *"Your wife will be like a fruitful vine within your
house."*[6] The vine keeper is called a husbandman. That's
what we are to be to our wives. For a vine to produce
good fruit it must be planted in good soil and tended
with care: with watering, pruning, and by feeding it with
nutrients. "

- *May your fountain be blessed, and may you rejoice in
the wife of your youth."*[7] Just as we enjoy the wife of
our youth if we provide her with love, affirm her, and
care for her, our enjoyment of our wife can increase into
old age.

- *"A wife of noble character is her husband's crown."*[8]
What we sow we reap. If we sow into our wife the same
attention and affirmation we gave during courtship, she
will glow with self-worth and security. Her radiance will
become like a crown to our head. A professor told the

---

[3] Ephesians 5:27
[4] Revelation 19
[5] 1 Corinthians 11:7
[6] Psalm 128:3
[7] Proverbs 5:18
[8] Proverbs 12:4

following story: A fellow professor was a handsome man, yet his wife was plain, almost homely. When I heard him speak highly of her, I wondered why such a good looking man would have married such a woman. When I was invited to their home for dinner I quickly learned the reason he married her. From the moment I entered their home his wife expressed grace and hospitality, looking after not only my comfort, but her husband's as well. She exuded an inner quality that expressed her love of life and others. Later I realized that her lack of outward beauty was insignificant compared to the beauty of her inner self. I also realized that the way her husband cherished her and praised her both directly and to others contributed to that inner quality that made her so appealing.

- *"He who finds a wife finds what is good and receives favor from the Lord."*[9] Here God is promising that He will bestow favor upon the man who lovingly cares for his wife. Conversely, as we noted earlier, Peter points out that if we don't treat our wife properly, our prayers will be hindered.[10]

- *"Enjoy life with your wife."*[11] One of the elements many couples let fall away in their marriage is having fun together. God intends that we have fun; we husbands can take the initiative to make it happen.

The Practical Application of This Passage

Our passage says that Jesus *"loved the church and gave Himself up for her that He might sanctify her,* **having cleansed her by the washing of water with the**

---

[9] Proverbs 18:22
[10] 1 Peter 3:7
[11] Ecclesiastes 9:9

word *[so] that He might present to Himself the church in all her glory." [Emphasis mine]*

Jesus' words wash us of our fears, our insecurities, and apprehensions. His words bring peace in the storms of life. His words wash us from all guilt and despair. His words are so powerful they can build faith in us. According to this passage, just as powerful as Christ's words are to the church, so a husband's words are powerful in the life of his wife. We are to minister love, encouragement, value, and security to our wives. We are to make our wife beautiful, lovely, and growing in godly character qualities—by means of our words and our actions toward her. We can ask ourself: *Am I in the process of making my wife what she was meant to be?* God created men to be the initiators. He created women to respond. Whatever we put into our marriage is what we get back. Let's keep in mind verse 27 *"that he might present [the church] to himself."*

Is my *church* radiant? Is she holy? Is she in glorious splendor? Is she faultless? Or have I made her to despair? I may be inclined to respond, "But you don't know *my* wife!" I must remember that I initiate, she responds. If my wife complains, I initiated it. If she is critical or negative, I'd better change my ways of relating to her.

Researchers have found that if a wife is unfaithful to her husband, it is usually because her husband has failed to meet her emotional needs, her sense of value and worth, and her need for intimacy and affection. When someone else comes along and meets those needs, she is vulnerable and may become unfaithful to her husband.

God intended that a husband and wife would enjoy one another. *"May your fountain be blessed, and may you rejoice in the wife of your youth.*"[12] *"Enjoy life with your wife, whom you love."*[13]

I was discipling a group of men in the church I was pastoring. I gave them a list of ninety-five character qualities from my wife's book[14] to keep in their wallets. They could refer to the list and return home from work each day prepared to affirm their wife with a character quality they appreciated in her.

What we've found is that when a person is affirmed for a positive quality, such as diligence, flexibility, or patience, even if it's only rarely demonstrated in that individual's life, the affirmation, if timely and sincere, makes them want to express that quality again. Eventually, by repetition, the positive quality is formed in their life and the negative fades away. We'll talk more about this in Chapter Fourteen.

Love Her as Your Own Body

*"So husbands ought also to love their own wives **as their own bodies**. He who loves his own wife loves himself; for no one ever hated his own flesh."*[15] *[Emphasis mine.]*

What a terrific thought! When I love my wife, I'm loving myself. I have found this to be true. The more I give of myself to my wife, the more love I get back. When I massage her aching neck and shoulders after she spends most of the day at the computer, she pours affection back on me. When I fix her a bowl of ice cream along with my own, she glows with admiration. When I see that she is not feeling well and I take the

---

[12] Proverbs 5:18
[13] Ecclesiastes 9:9
[14] *Developing Godly Character in Children*, by Beverly Caruso, Ken Marks, and Debbie Peterson, Hands to Help Publishing.
[15] Ephesians 5:28

43

initiative to prepare dinner or clean up the kitchen, I am rewarded with growing respect. Any love I extend to her comes back to me—with interest.

This giving and receiving of love benefits even our health. Dr. Walt Larimore writes: "Married people are not only more likely to live longer, but they are also more satisfied with living and seem to better survive a variety of diseases."[16]

This whole thing started in the Garden of Eden. God told Adam to give each of the animals a name. I can picture the scene: "That one looks like a chimpanzee. You look like an alligator. And you, you look like a giraffe. But wait a minute. There's at least two of each of you guys. You have each other. I don't have anybody like me. I need a partner too."

After a while Adam got tired of thinking up names. He got sleepy and took a nap. That's when God did some surgery and removed Adam's rib. God said that it was, *"not good that the man should be alone; I will make him an help meet for him."*[17]

When Adam woke up, he found he was married. The King James Bible tells us Adam said, *'This is now bone of my bones and flesh of my flesh.'*[18] The Living Bible quotes him as saying, *"At last!"* In today's English it would be more like, "Wow man! This is it!"

Could Adam have rejected this beautiful being? Could he have said, "No way! I don't want to be tied down to her." Why would he want to? She came from him, she was a part of him. *"She shall be called 'woman' for she was taken out of man."*[19]

---

[16] Taken from His Brain, Her Brain by Walt Larimore, M.D. Copyright ©1988 by Zondervan. Used by permission of Zondervan.
[17] Genesis 2:18
[18] Genesis 2:23
[19] Genesis 2:23

Woman was created from the rib of man,
Not from his head to top him,
Nor from his feet to be walked upon.
She was made from his side to be his equal.
From beneath his arm to be protected by him,
From very near his heart to be loved by him.

Author unknown

The Hebrew word *succour* used in the original Hebrew for *helpmeet* in the telling of this story, gives us a glimpse of God's perspective of the role of the wife. When God said, "I will make him a helpmeet," He was using a word meaning "one who saves another from extremity. One who gives help or relief when another is in danger, one who affords relief. It is a word showing an action as one who gives water to one dying of thirst. Or who puts a tourniquet around one bleeding to death."[20]

God was telling us that Eve was not a subordinate servant. Rather, she would release her husband from his aloneness and incompleteness. She would save him from his self-absorption and ineffectiveness, his inefficiency. Every other biblical use of this term *succour* is used to describe God's saving action toward His people, saving the nation of Israel. God created our wives to be far more than a mere helper or servant. She is our completer—our Father's perfect design and gift for us. She is an ally, an accomplice, or comrade. God was responding to a need He created into the man, before Adam knew he had the need.[21]

---

[20] From a televised message. The authors regret that the speaker's name cannot be provided.
[21] From the previously mentioned televised message. The authors regret that the speaker's name cannot be provided.

How Are We to Love Our Wives?

Most husbands want their wives to feel loved—truly loved. The story is told of the wife who whined, "We've been married now for nearly twenty years and you never tell me you love me."

Her husband barked back, "I told you twenty years ago that I loved you, and that still stands for today."

Of course, most of us know that women want to hear those three little words often, every day. Saying it isn't enough though. A woman feels loved when we do the things that mean love to her. One of those is showing affection. And affection can mean different things to different women. We'd be wise to ask our wife what specifically means affection to her. We'll be taking a closer look at *affection* in Chapter Fourteen.

Nourish Her

"So husbands ought also to love their own wives as their own bodies. He who loves his own wife loves himself; for no one ever hated his own flesh, but **nourishes** *and cherishes it, just as Christ also does the church."*[22] "The word *nourish* in the original Greek of the New Testament means 'to carefully feed and love' – 'to see that every need is met.' The Greek word for Savior is 'provider of all things.' We as husbands can be a savior to our wife—a provider of all things.

Protection is in this word. It's easy to understand how houseplants differ. Some will die if they get too much sunshine or water. Others will die if they don't get enough. We husbands can study our own wife to learn her specific needs, then we can set out to nurture her accordingly.

---

[22] Ephesians 5:29 New American Standard Bible

Cherish Her

*"So husbands ought also...**to cherish her**...just as Christ also does the church."*[23] The Greek word *anthenems* translated *to cherish* in English means "to highly value; to take great care and concern; to protect with tender care." In *His Brain, Her Brain*, Dr. Walt Larimore, writes: "We will develop strong feelings for whatever we treasure. Psychological studies show that when a person makes a decision to honor and value something, his or her feelings will start to change within six weeks."[24]

Dr. Larimore expands this thought:[25]

"One day I was in the physicians' lounge of our local hospital, having a cup of coffee with a psychiatrist friend named Peter who had grown up in Greece. Peter was my local expert in the Greek language, so I asked him how he interpreted the Greek word *anthenems*.

"As he explained the various descriptions of the word to me, I was pleasantly surprised to discover a much richer and deeper meaning. He said this term could be used to describe

- the most fragile and valuable art,
- the most delicate and costly bone china, porcelain vase, and
- the most valuable and exquisite jewelry

"He went on to say that the term is used to describe a dainty, delicate, luxurious, ethereal, or subtle but extremely rare and dear gift—priceless pieces of beautiful artistry, belongings of immense and incredible important, worth, and value.

---

[23] Ephesians 5:29a

[24] Taken from His Brain, Her Brain by Walt Larimore, M.D. Copyright ©1988 by Zondervan. Used by permission of Zondervan.

[25] Ibid

"These artworks are designed, intended, and crafted to be appreciated, beloved, and desired; to be honored, esteemed, and valued, to be respected, and protected; to be sheltered, shielded, and praised; to be proclaimed, lifted up, and spotlighted; and to be polished, displayed, and treasured."

Wow! This opened my eyes to the fact that the Bible is saying that God has built for and given to each of us husbands a priceless and delicate treasure—our wife—to care for, value, and esteem.

If you're married, God has given you a spouse whom He intended and created for you—a woman of indescribable, inconceivable, and incredible value.

And men, the owner of the art gallery—our heavenly Father—holds us responsible for our wives' care. He holds us responsible for caring for and caring deeply about them.

Back in early history Satan took this precious gift God had created for man and devalued it. He turned woman into something for men to own, to use, and abuse. His plan was that the beauty of marriage, the potential of that wonderful teamwork and partnership, would be undermined so that men would view women as little more than animals, something to use for his own convenience and pleasure. A servant, merely to cook for him, care for his home, reproduce children, and use as an object of lust.

I wonder how we would change the way we value our wife if we truly had God's view of her. Would we value her more highly than any of our possessions; even more highly than our profession? If we own something of great value such as a classic car, we take special care of it. We park it in the garage and keep it clean and waxed. We guard it from getting scratched by the children's bikes or the lawn mower. A proverb asks *"An excellent wife, who can find? For her worth is far above jewels. "*[26]

Love Includes Touch

Touch is an important element of life and of marital love—especially for a woman. Kissing; hugging; stroking, massaging. Each of these communicates love to our wife. Touch promotes health, both physical and emotional health. Bev discusses many benefits of the healing power of touch in her book *God's Gift of Friendship - Tools for Improving Relationships.* Let me share some additional benefits:

Within the marriage, touch is a vital fuel for keeping the fires of love aflame. As newlyweds Bev and I noticed with warm amusement the way her grandparents publicly expressed their affection. When they were seated, Grandpa's hand usually rested on Grandma's leg. He would lightly pat her several times every now and then. Sometimes she would respond by patting his arm. As young lovers Bev and I enjoyed stroking each others' hands, arm or neck, and wondered about Grandma and Grandpa's love pats. As we've grown older together, Bev and I now sometimes laugh at ourselves. We now pat nearly as much as we stroke. We wonder if perhaps the stroke is more a sensual loving touch and patting more a reassuring one—for both the patted and the patter.

For a woman, touching is a big part of affection, not as a prelude to sex, but *just because*…. It's that way in every culture. Women love to hug. They hug their children, their pets, their stuffed animals, their pillows. A husband can cultivate an environment of affection when he hugs his wife—often. It sends an important message: "You are important to me; I'll protect you: I'm

---

[26] Proverbs 31:10 New American Standard Bible

proud of you; I want to be close to you; I'm happy with you." All those things can be said with one little hug.

A study at the University of California at Los Angeles[27] (UCLA) found that the average woman needs 8 to 10 meaningful touches every day from someone she cares about in order to remain emotionally and physically healthy. They also discovered that possibly men could add up to two years to their own lives if only they would take the time at the beginning and end of their day to give their wives a lingering hug.

A team from the University of North Carolina studied the effects of hugging on both partners in 38 couples. The study showed hugs increased levels of oxytocin, a *bonding* hormone, and reduced blood pressure, which cuts the risk of heart disease. Both men and women in loving relationships were found to have higher levels of the hormone than others after a hug. But the study also found all women had reduced levels of cortisol following the hug, as well as reporting the blood pressure benefits. [28]

A group of psychologists, physicians and insurance companies undertook a research project to determine the secret of long life and success, and discovered that kissing one's wife before going to work can greatly increase the likelihood of longevity and success! Those who smooch their wives in the morning had fewer car accidents, missed less work due to illness, and earned 20 to 30 percent more money than their non-kissing counterparts.

Researcher Dr. Arthur Szabo offers this reason for the increased benefit of kissing, "A husband who kisses his wife every morning begins the day with a positive

---

[27] Cited by Gary Smalley in his video series, *Hidden Keys to Loving Relationships*.
[28] BBC News, August 8, 2005

attitude." It's great to know that something so enjoyable is good for you too! Overall, men who kiss in the morning live an average of five years longer than men who are stingy with their kisses. Isn't that great? Everybody wins when Dad kisses Mom.[29]

Try a Cup of Kindness

"Love is kind."[30] Kindness is fairly easy to practice in the workplace where we want to make a good impression. Yet it should be seen first and most in the home, toward our wife and children.

I love the description of kindness the Apostle James described, it's a good description of how a man should lead his family: *"Wisdom that comes from Heaven is first of all pure and full of quiet gentleness, then it is peace loving and courteous. It allows discussion and is willing to yield to others; it is full of mercy and good deeds. It is whole hearted and straightforward and sincere."*[31] The Apostle Paul, wrote: *"Have kind affection one to another, in honor preferring one another."*[32] And again, *"Put on mercy, kindness, humility, meekness, patience."*[33] True humility is recognizing our position, but taking a lower place.

It's clear that our wives need strong leaders who are also compassionate. If we are all strength and toughness, and treat our wife harshly, with sarcastic teasing, if we're rude and domineering, our wife will be downcast, unresponsive in lovemaking, and generally miserable. If we love our wife as Christ loves the church—she will love us in return, her respect will come from her heart,

---

[29] Study headed by Dr. Arthur Szabo, Dean, Faculty of Science, Wilfrid Lauier University.
[30] 1 Corinthians 13:4
[31] James 3:17 Living Bible
[32] Romans 12:10
[33] Colossians 3:12

not out of obligation. She will want to follow our leadership.

Let's take a look at our text passage as a whole now, in light of the things we've discussed.

> *"Submit to one another out of reverence for Christ. Wives, submit to your husbands as to the Lord. For the husband is the head of the wife, as Christ is the head of the church, his body, of which he is the Savior.*
>
> *Now as the church submits to Christ, so also wives should submit to their husbands in everything.*
>
> *Husbands, love your wives, just as Christ loved the church and gave himself up for her to make her holy, cleansing her by the washing with water through the word, and to present her to himself as a radiant church, without stain or wrinkle or any other blemish, but holy and blameless.*
>
> *In this same way, husbands ought to love their wives as their own bodies. He who loves his wife loves himself. After all, no one ever hated his own body, but he feeds and cares for it, just as Christ does the church— for we are members of his body.*
>
> *For this reason a man will leave his father and mother and be united to his wife, and the two will become one flesh." This is a profound mystery—but I am talking about Christ and the church.*
>
> *However, each one of you also must love his wife as he loves himself, and the wife must respect her husband."*[34]

---

[34] Ephesians 5:21-33

Our passage ends with the wife's response to her husband's love. Bev will resume her narrative now, with some insight for wives.

Keeping It Fresh

Chapter Seven

We're Each on a Cycle – But Which One?

"Each one of you also must love his wife as he loves himself, ***and the wife must respect her husband."***[1] (*Emphasis mine.*)

Most of us women want to be loved with that agape kind of love that Pete has been addressing. Our text verse above ends by saying we *"must respect"* our husband.

God created women so that our greatest need is to know we are loved. In the same way, a man's greatest need is to know he is respected. Instead, we women generally focus on loving our husband—when what he needs most is our respect. The Old Testament queen, Vashti, made this mistake. King Xerxes was hosting his friends at a feast. His wife refused to come when he summoned her. The king became furious and banned her from his presence for the rest of her life. He knew that if she got away with it, the queen's conduct would become known to all the women, and so they would despise their husbands and follow Vashti's example. What was really at stake here? Respect! Not only for the king, but for all men in the eyes of their wives.[2]

---

[1] Ephesians 5:33
[2] Esther chapter 1

No one calls her selfish or self-centered if a woman says, "I just want someone to love me, to make me feel special, to make me the most important person in his life." It sounds natural for a woman to want that. What if a man said, "I just want someone to respect me, to make me feel special, to make me feel the most honored person in her life?" That's how men feel, but they don't dare voice it. Yet men do what they do for the admiration of that one woman. If she doesn't admire him, 85% of men will withdraw—that's the honorable thing to do. They become silent, say nothing, and go off by themselves.[3]

If a man senses his wife doesn't respect him, it doesn't matter much to know his wife loves him. It's quite simple: without respect from his wife, he can't love her properly. And if he doesn't love her properly, she will not receive from him the tender love she longs for. Most English versions of the Bible translate this word as *reverence* rather than *respect*. The original Greek meaning is *"to reverence, venerate, to treat with deference or reverential obedience."* It is that attitude of heart that we normally hold for those in authority, or who are older than ourselves.

If we were expecting a visit to our home from a dignitary, perhaps a member of a royal family, we wouldn't welcome them to a dirty house or greet them wearing the clothes we wore while working in the garden. Nor would we speak as though speaking to a child or to an old childhood playmate. Instead we would present ourselves with decorum, showing honor to our guest out of respect for their office or position. It's with that same attitude that we should view our husband. He can be our best friend, but he also holds a God-designated office. As his wife, we will know all his

---

[3] *Keys to Loving Relationships* video series, by Gary Smalley

weaknesses, even his eccentricities. Yet we can extend to him respect, reverence, and honor in our words, our actions, and our tone.

In response to our respect—our reverence—for our husband, his love for us will grow and he will be more inclined to openly show his love in return. As a result of that expression of love, our respect for him will grow. It truly is reciprocal—respect generates love which generates respect and on it goes.

Without that respect, a husband feels less than a man. He feels diminished in his own home—the very place where respect is most treasured by a man. He responds then, by withholding the very thing we need most from him—his love. Deprived of love, we lose respect for him. A negative cycle is at work.[4]

Boys Who Never Grew Up
Dennis and Barbara Rainey teach that God designed a man to pass through five stages during his lifetime:[5]

Boyhood
Adolescence
Manhood
Mentor
Patriarch

The Raineys point out that it is to be a process in order for him to become the man God intends him to be. Many men marry and have children, but they never truly reach manhood. "The question we could ask about many men today is: "Will he leave adolescence behind?" Real men are not born," the Raineys point out, "they're

---

[4] For an in depth study of this concept, see *Love and Respect,* by Emerson Eggerichs, Thomas Nelson, 2004
[5] From a Family Life Today Radio Series, taught by Dennis and Barbara Rainey.

made." A man needs a woman who believes in him and knows the goal.

It's easy for us wives to hinder the process by:

- **Feeding his childishness** - We're told *"Do not repay evil with evil or insult with insult, but with blessing."*[6] When we do we're acting on a childish level. We need to choose to grow up ourselves, to guard our words and our actions. In doing so we will help our husband to grow up too.

- **Enabling him in his weaknesses and failures -** *"Make no provision for the flesh."*[7] Do we feed his weaknesses? Do we make excuses for him? Or lie to his boss? Do we stock the fridge with what he shouldn't have?

- **Treating him like a child** - *"Do not think of yourselves more highly than you ought."*[8] We can ask: "Am I thinking wrongly about myself, therefore less of him?"

- **Having negative expectations** - We can subtly communicate to him, "You'll never be the spiritual leader of our family." Of course he isn't perfect; he will make mistakes. But we mustn't give up on him. We can believe the best, not the worst of our husband, lest we make ourself a prophetess by having negative expectations.

- **Turning his heart away from God** - We need to guard ourselves. Solomon's wives turned his heart away

---

[6] 1 Peter 3:9
[7] Romans 13:14 New American Standard Bible
[8] Romans 12:3

from God. Then there was Ahab: *"There was never anyone like Ahab, who sold himself to do evil in the eyes of the LORD,* **urged on by Jezebel his wife.***"*[9] [*Emphasis mine.*]

The result of making the above mistakes will be a husband unworthy of the respect we've been talking about.

We may be married to such a man; we may be married to a godly man. Regardless, we are told to respect him.

The bottom line is that a man has three basic needs: acceptance, approval, and appreciation. If we supply these three, we'll have a happy man. In order to meet these needs, our heart must be filled with respect, not because he's earned it, but because we've chosen to respect him.

There are many aspects to being respectful of our husband. Respect is not something to paste on our face, or force into our words and voice. It must come from our heart—a conscious choice which produces an ongoing attitude. I see this being worked out in a number of ways in a marriage.

Respect Him by Accepting Him As He Is

The instinct that God built into us women to mother is sometimes hard to control. We are not our husband's mother. One man wrote: "One thing I wish my wife understood is that constant criticism does NOT inspire me to greater love. How it frustrates me to sincerely want to make her happy and please her. But so often I try to do loving things for her, and I'm met with criticism ('you're not doing it right; my way...')." If we're breaking down our man's ego at home, there is

---

[9] 1 Kings 21:25 Today's New International Version

quite likely another woman out there willing to build him up.[10]

One important aspect of respecting our husband is the example we set for the following generations. Our role modeling may just mean the difference between our children having successful marriages or ultimate divorce.

Respect Him by Affirming Him and Letting Him Know He Is Admired

It's so easy to let our husband know the things about him we want him to change, the things we don't like. He could probably write the list himself after all our complaining. That complaining or even a look of derision can erode our husband's sense of worth. What he needs to know is that we notice the good in him. We admire his physical strength, his job skills, his people skills, or his spiritual growth. We appreciate that he's a hard worker, a good breadwinner, that we value his loyalty, his friendship. Anything that communicates to him that we're feeling: "That's my man!" If he's matured, grown spiritually, or overcome areas of weakness, we can let him know that we've noticed. When he gives of himself selflessly, we can praise him. All of these are like vitamins to his soul. We can set as a goal to tell him something we admire about him–every day.[11]

Respect Him by Cooperating with Him.

Our husband is God's delegated leader for us—our head. If we do not follow, he cannot lead. We are to fit

---

[10] Candice Atherton

[11] See the full chapter on Affirmation in our book on relationships titled: *God's Gift of Friendship – Tools for Improving Relationships*, available from the authors at: www.PeteandBevCaruso.com.

into our husband's plans, not oppose him, conflict with him, or compete with him. Many women feel frustrated by the confines of home responsibilities. We may need to hold down that job, or we may have a longing to work outside the home, or to have a ministry of our own. These are appropriate if we have our priorities in order. God made us to be a helpmeet for our husband. He is our primary responsibility and ministry. We can meet his needs first: spiritually, mentally and physically. We'll have to guard against letting the needs of children, the church, our job, our extended family, or our friends come before this God-given role. Only then can we expect God's blessing upon our work or ministry.

Respect Him by Getting Rid of Unreal Expectations

We would not attempt to change a friend into someone she is not. Why do we expect to change our husband? All men are not alike. They don't all love sports and hate shopping. Much of our disappointment in life is because we have imagined what can never be. We can make it a matter of prayer and conscious effort to set aside our expectations that he cannot live up to.

Respect Him by Being Patient with Him

Our husband is in the process of learning to be priest, lover, father, provider and friend, just as we are learning to be helper, lover, mother, homemaker and friend. I like the button that says: PBPWMGINFWMY.[12] Patience is not just holding our tongue. It includes keeping our attitude right. Our words may be gentle, our voice at a quiet volume, but the tone of our voice can be screaming, "You idiot, why don't you get your act together!" It

---

[12] Please Be Patient With Me, God Is Not Finished With Me Yet

could just be that our own attitude is the source of our husband's bad attitude and actions.

Respect Him by Forgiving His Past Mistakes

If our attitude is right, we'll forgive his mistakes and errors. That's especially hard for us women. Bringing up his past mistakes only helps to erode our marriage. We can choose to forgive our husband and commit to never bring up those issues again. Then we can forgive each new wrong and let it be forgotten.

Respect Him by Expressing Appreciation

As wives we can express gratefulness for not only what he does in providing for the family, his physical work around the home, his time and attention for us and the children, but also for what he refrains from doing. If we reset our expectations to zero each day, we will be grateful for any kindness shown or any small thing given to us. By looking for things to be grateful for in our husband, we can eliminate the attitude of criticism from our heart.

Respect Him by Praying For and With Him

No one knows a husband and his needs better than his wife. What a privilege we wives have to take those needs to our Heavenly Father. He awaits our requests on our husband's behalf.

We may have longed for our husband to spend time with us in prayer on a regular basis. If he doesn't do so, we have every right to ask God to give him the desire. A word of caution, though: we must guard against expecting our husband to fill those needs in our life that only God can fill. God wants each individual to have our own relationship with Him regardless of how close our husband may or may not be to Him.

Respect Him by Learning How to *Appeal* to Him

Sometimes a husband goes beyond his limitations, or sets upon a course of action that we believe will lead to problems for the family. There is a biblical pattern for appealing to one in authority.[13] We have the right and responsibility to follow it. It starts with prayer. Then in meekness and humility, being mindful of our tone of voice, we can state our concerns without condemnation, judging or belittling. Then we step back and leave things in God's hands. God knows whether to stop our husband or to let him fall on his face in failure. Sometimes allowing failure is God's way of getting one's attention.

Respect Him by Staying on Our Own Side of the Net

It's so easy to get carried away in our desire to see our husband learn his God-given role. Or is it that we want him to husband us *in the way* we want him to? Either way, that is not what God wants of us. I like to think of marriage as a game of tennis between two friends. Each player has his own part to play to keep the game moving. If one player focuses on how the other is playing, that one stops playing his or her own best. Both the husband and wife need to focus on their own side of the net, drawing upon God to teach us our skills.

Respect Him by Being Interested in His Interests

A great way to strengthen our marriage is to share mutual interests with our husband. Yet many wives have no desire to share their husband's love of football, or gardening, or hunting. We can ask the Lord to give us a willingness to learn a little about our husband's interest. Ask questions; read about the subject. We may be surprised that we can at least become knowledgeable

---

[13] 1 Timothy 5:1

enough to discuss a topic intelligently with him. My friend Ashley did this. Her husband loved anything to do with computers. She hated following Chris around computer stores and feeling lonely when he spent hours, not only at his own computer, but helping others with theirs. Finally she decided to learn a little about his hobby. She was amazed that it wasn't as boring or difficult as it seemed. Before long she was locating old friends, chatting online—and loving it.

Respect Him by Being Supportive

A man needs to be able to bare his soul to his wife, about his faith, his work, his family, his worries—without criticism. Men get tired of having to be the tough guy, the strong one. Sometimes they need room to feel sad or discouraged without being made to feel like a failure. Yet if his wife is demeaning at such times, or if she tells others about his low times, he won't feel safe about sharing this part of his life. One husband wrote, "Frequently, when I get angry over something she has said or done and have the temerity to express my feelings, she just dismisses it as me being overtired, or some other trite toss-off. This is akin to a guy seeing a woman angry and saying sarcastically, 'Guess it's that time of the month again!'"[14]

Respect Him by Letting Him Have Friends

Just as we enjoy being with other women for female companionship, our husband needs to spend time with other men. *"As iron sharpens iron, so a man sharpens the countenance of his friend."*[15] Our attitude about the time he spends with his friends can bless him or cause

---

[14] *The Proper Care and Feeding of Husbands*, by Dr. Laura Schlessinger, Harper Collins Publishers, 2004.
[15] Proverbs 27:17 Amplified Bible

him to feel like an animal let out of its cage—and not wanting to return to it. A marriage is enriched when both spouses are free to pursue outside interests and friends.

Respect Him by Appreciating His Background and Family

Whatever our husband's natural abilities are, we can choose to accept them. He may not have the educational level we would have liked. In addition, other influences have brought him to his current place and maturity level. We can long for things to be different, but they aren't.

When we get married, in a very real sense, we also marry our husband's family. They are an integral part of his personality and life. The things that attracted us to him are results, to a great extent, of their influence on him. We may not like his family members as individuals, or collectively for that matter, but we can learn to love them through the grace Jesus provides, if we ask *Him*. Whether they are of a different culture from ours, or the family next door that we've known all our life, they have different ways of thinking and doing things. By choosing to, we can accept those differences and incorporate as much as we comfortably can of their ways into our family life.

By making a conscious choice to accept all that has brought him to what and who he is now, we can bring a peace and joy into our relationship and into our home. This will free him from the stereotypes we brought into our marriage and release him to be who he is, not who we thought we married, or who we hope he'll someday become.

Respect Him by Honoring His Role as Priest of the Home

It's the nature of women to be sensitive to things in the spiritual realm. As a result, we can find ourselves getting ahead of our husbands in spiritual matters.

Jill was a dear friend from my childhood—a stay-at-home mom. One day Jill told me she was disappointed that her husband was not taking the spiritual leadership in their family. After discussing it together, we realized that she had time to go to mid-week Bible studies, to attend Christian conferences, and to study her Bible. Her husband did not. She was growing in her love for the Lord and loved to talk about Him. Her husband's personality was more subdued.

Jill decided that perhaps her husband simply didn't want to compete with her as the spiritual leader of their family. She chose to be less verbal about the things she was learning; not that she would stop growing, just less talkative.

To her amazement she soon saw her husband taking the active lead as the priest in their home. "He has a much deeper walk with God than I ever imagined," she told me a few months later.

Even if we aren't spending regular time as a couple in prayer, if a wife will draw upon her husband for his priestly role at the moment of need, most men will respond accordingly. When one of the children is hurt; when finances are low; or when we are discouraged, we can take the opportunity to request humbly, without a self-righteous attitude, for our husband to pray about the specific need of the moment. We may be surprised by his response as my friend Marsha was. Her husband was an unbeliever who often mocked her and fought against her efforts to teach their children about God. One day she decided to call upon his priestly role anyway. She stopped him that day and asked him to pray for her headache. He laid his hand on her head. She waited with eyes closed, in silence. After a few moments they each went on their way—and her headache went away. Some time after that her husband became a believer too.

Respect Him by Taking Care of Ourself

Twenty-First Century women tend to try to 'be all' to everyone. We have our career, our hobbies, our friends and our lovely homes. At the end of the day we're so exhausted we tend to resent the needs of our husband. On her daily call-in radio show, Dr. Laura Schlessinger responded to the complaints of just such a wife. "It's your obligation to keep yourself healthy and fit so that you can be involved with your husband. You can't do the "I am tired" bit every day and have your husband just accept that this important, intimate part of his life is simply going to be controlled by your whim. It is your obligation not to be tired all the time. So take a nap, eat more protein, take your vitamins. What kind of thing is that to pull on him? What if he said, "I'm too tired and I'm not going to work anymore"? You have obligations to each other, and one of them is not to be constantly tired. That is not an acceptable excuse. Your commitments outside your marriage are too much for you. This is making you somewhat hostile and negative to the intimacy that is a great joy and blessing in a relationship. It's one thing to have a tiring, stressful day—or even week. It's another thing to allow outside activities, no matter how seemingly important, to routinely get in the way of obligations to the roles created by holy vows, moral obligations, and love."[16]

---

[16] *The Proper Care and Feeding of Husbands*, by Dr. Laura Schlessinger, Harper Collins Publishers, 2004.

Respect Him by Freeing Him to Love in His Own Way

Sometimes I find myself struggling to make the choice to accept and respect Pete, not because he's lacking as a husband, but because I still have so much to learn about being a good wife. But I've found that by choosing to practice these seventeen elements of respect, Pete is free to shower me with the love that I so dearly need. I've truly received from Pete an unconditional love that reflects in human form the love that Jesus has for His church.

This makes me want to return, not only respect, but love, to Pete. It was this love that the Apostle Paul was writing about when he gave instructions to the young pastor Titus, with instructions to set in order the church on the Island of Crete.

Chapter Eight

Love Him Like a Friend

Love is always a decision. Whether it is love between parent and child, between husband and wife, or between two friends—love is a choice.

Paul told men to love their wives with affectionate, sacrificial love—*Agape love*—as Pete described in Chapter Five. Titus used a different Greek word when he told the older women to teach the younger to *"love their husbands."*[1] This word, *philos*, comes from the same root word for the name of our American city of Philadelphia, the City of Brotherly Love. It means *"to be a friend, associate, or even a groomsman."*[2] In the Gospels, Jesus used *agape* five times for each single use of *philos or phileo.* Why did Titus not use the same word for a woman's love of her husband as Paul did for the man's love of his wife? To me it indicates that Christian women will naturally love their husbands with *agape* love. What we need to learn is to be a friend to him.

Titus is teaching us that women need to be taught to love their husband as a friend—it doesn't come naturally.

---

[1] Titus 2:4
[2] Strong's Concordance

69

Keeping It Fresh

Dr. Laura Schlessinger writes: "So many young women are products of divorce or never created homes, were neglected by career mothers, were indoctrinated by the anti-family feminists throughout their schooling, and are surrounded by a culture that glorifies selfish gratification over sacrifice, it's no wonder so many of them are 'surprised" to not only hear of their obligations to husbands and children, but are also amazed at the gratification derived from doing so."[3]

Love Him by Being His Friend

How can we love our husband with *philos* love? Not by playing a mother-role in his life. He doesn't need a mom; he needs a friend. If we've only been viewing that guy on the other pillow as a man and a lover, we're missing a lot of the fun part of marriage that God intended for us. Let's see how we can work at becoming his friend.

Love Him by Having Fun with Him

If we don't know how to relax and have fun, we can start by praying about it. We can also ask our husband to help us to learn. And we can make a conscious choice and effort to become a playful, fun person to be with. Even after fifty years together, Pete and I can still have fun by sneaking up to pour a glass of cold water over the shower door, or hiding behind the bedroom door in the "all together," or taking the day to lie together on a blanket beside our nearby lake and find images in the clouds.

---

[3] *The Proper Care and Feeding of Husbands*, by Dr. Laura Schlessinger, Harper Collins Publishers, 2004.

Love Him by Letting Him Know We Like *Him*

There is a difference between *loving* and *liking* someone. We may assume our husband knows we like him, but unless we show it by our words and actions he may wonder, just as we wonder whether he loves us unless he tells us so. Whereas we women receive positive emotional strokes from our family and friends, most men lack this emotional support from others. Our husband probably needs this kind of support from us far more than we need it from him.

Love Him by Being Mindful When to Switch Hats

We may work with our husband on a daily basis. I do! Pete and I share an office as well as our ministry. But we don't have to carry that business relationship into our private interaction. Even a young wife can take off her *Mommy Hat* at times. About the only time we should not readily just *change hats* for our husband when we're at home is when a nursing baby needs to eat, a child is sick, or under similar circumstances. We can learn to readily take off those many hats and turn our attention to being a loving, affectionate, responsive wife and friend.

Love Him by Being Willing to be Spontaneous

I don't mean that we should fill our social calendar without his knowledge. Still, we can be as prepared as possible to go with him when he says, "Let's go!" Many men don't plan outings ahead of time. Yet we wives can miss out because we are unwilling to turn off the stove and serve the meal the next night, or to go out with our hair or makeup less than perfect. Married couples frequently dismiss the idea of spur-of-the-moment-dates because they lack available babysitters. When our children were small, I tried to have at least two sitters who were willing to respond on short notice. If one was not available, perhaps the other would be. Some couples make arrangements with another couple to be available for each other on short notice.

Love Him by Being Attractive For Him

Let's face it, if we're going out with our friends or having them in for a time together we dress nicely and arrange our hair and face. We can become the wife of our husband's dreams–or are we the wife of his nightmares? We can evaluate our hair—in a style he likes; our clothing—according to his provision and tastes; our person—is he proud to be seen together? (Think weight, neatness, a meek and quiet spirit, etc.); and our home—does it reflect his standard of living, tastes and ideas of comfort?

Love Him by Cheering Him On and Encouraging Him When He's Down

Just as there are times when we wives need to be encouraged or comforted, so our husband needs our emotional support. We must take care, though, to comfort him as a wife, not like a mother. Our encouragement should result in his feeling he can overcome the problem as a man. Motherly encouragement may leave him feeling like a little boy.

There are times when any husband can feel that everyone is against him; that nothing is going right. He should know that our loyalty to him is not based on his success, nor can it be lost because of failure. We can be his cheering section and let him know we believe in him.

One man wrote, "The world is full of messages to men that there are standards we don't meet. There is always another man more handsome, more virile, or more athletic than we are. None of that matters if the most important person in our life looks up to us, accepts us as we are, and loves us even though we aren't perfect. Maybe there is a part of the small boy that never leaves the grown man, I don't know. All I know is that the husband who has a wife who supports him and praises him for the positive things he does is the envy of all the other men who have to live with criticism, sarcasm, and constant reminders of their failings."[4]

Love Him by Being a Teammate to Him

Although we are to love our husband as one friend loves another, he is also our partner. We can look for ways we can complete our husband. That's part of the meaning of the word in Genesis when God said, *"I will make a* helpmeet *for him."*[5] [*Emphasis mine*]

Love Him by Giving Affection that's Not Connected to Sex

Some women are surprised to learn that men can enjoy affection without sex. The problem is that the guys often misread our affectionate moves. We can talk about this subject with him, letting him know there are times we just want to show affection, but not necessarily receive it, without it leading to anything else. Some couples work out a code or signal that she can use to express which kind of affection she is showing.

Love Him by Communicating with Him

"Speaking the truth in love, ...let no corrupt communication proceed out of your mouth, but that which is good to the use of edifying, that it may minister grace unto the hearers."[6] *"Let your speech be always*

---

[4] *The Proper Care and Feeding of Husbands*, by Dr. Laura Schlessinger, Harper Collins Publishers, 2004.
[5] Genesis 2:18
[6] Ephesians 15:29

with grace, seasoned with salt, that you may know how you ought to answer every man."[7] We gals love to communicate. We talk to our girlfriends, our sisters, and anyone else who will listen. Learning to communicate with our husband is worth the effort. We can start by telling him calmly and clearly what we're feeling, instead of what many wives do. They expect him to lovingly draw it out of her after she slams the cupboard door or thumps the coffee cup on the table in front of him. Few men respond favorably to this form of communication. What we want is love and concern from our husband. Of course choosing the right time, and the right setting is important as well.

Our husband has a great need to really know his wife. In fact, the scripture teaches him to live with us according to understanding. How is he going to understand us if we don't share who we are—if we aren't transparent. As a wife, we can be:

- understood for who really we are
- understood for what we are doing and why
- understood for how we feel about things
- understood for what our goals are
- understood for the fears that we have

Honesty and openness are a vital part of a marriage. Our husband should feel confident that we have no secrets from him. Such a man will be secure in his relationship with his wife. Of course we need a little privacy. But if we're not open and honest, we'll get a lot of questions like:

- Where have you been?
- What were you doing?
- What's the matter?

---

[7] Colossians 4:6

This only results in us feeling that he is prying and nagging.

If we are struggling in some area of our life, we can tell him so. If things aren't going well with the children or on our job, we can voluntarily tell him about it. We don't have to go into detail, but we can keep him informed. If we don't tell him these things, he will sense that we're holding back. Without knowing what it is that's bothering us, he'll imagine things. Probably the wrong things.

We're instructed to *"speak the truth in love"* to him.[8] The painful truth is better than the insecurity of half truths or hidden truths. On the other hand, we should not expect to know what our husband is doing all the time. He's not accountable to us for his privacy, nor for his relationship with God.

Love Him by Choosing to Believe in Him

Believe that he has goodwill in his heart for us. He may be clumsy in the way he shows that love. He may not love in the way we want to be loved. But he's probably doing the best he knows how. We can love our husband by believing he has the best intentions toward us.

God intended that loving our husband would be the most satisfying and fulfilling role we women would have. If it is not, we can make whatever adjustments necessary to see that it is.

Learning to love our husband like a friend is definitely rewarding. Pete is my best friend. That reality didn't come easily, but it's been well worth the cultivation of this friendship that has lasted half a

---

[8] Ephesians 4:15

century. As best friends we've had to work through the whole area of equality and authority.

Chapter Nine

What's the Big Deal About Authority?

Two of the most misunderstood aspects of marriage are the principles of equality and authority. In the secular world, just as it is regarding submission, the idea of authority having any place in a contemporary marriage is considered passé—old fashioned. As Christian couples, though, we need to take a close look at what God has to say about authority.

God Created Marriage

It was God's idea to make man and to place a woman beside him. Not as his competitor. Not inferior or superior; but his equal. As I (Pete) pointed out in Chapter Six, God knew that Adam was lonely. He was incomplete. So God put him to sleep and took from his side an equal partner. She was to be his companion, his friend, and his co-heir to the glory of God. She was to complete him, not compete with him.

This equality was not a new concept for God. He was already part of an equality that had existed since eternity past. God the Father, God the Son, and God the Holy Spirit were always equal, and forever will continue to be. They are ONE, yet they exist as three distinct personalities. This plurality is clear, for God said, *"Let*

*us make man in **our** image."[1] [Emphasis mine]* In the
New Testament we see Jesus as one aspect of that
plurality. *"In the beginning was the Word, and the Word
was with God, and the Word was God."[2]* They are not
three gods, they are merely one God evident in three
personalities and known by their titles: Father, Son, and
Holy Spirit, and known collectively as the Trinity. How
are they One?

In each of their attributes they are equal. They are
one in equality; yet they are all God. They are one in
their divinity. They are one in unity; they cannot
disagree. There was no argument in heaven about which
of them would become a man. They were in perfect
harmony.

We read of Jesus in Philippians, *"Who, being in very
nature God, did not consider equality with God something to be grasped."[3]* Paul is saying that Jesus didn't
cling to His divinity. He willingly, temporarily, set aside
His omnipresence, His omnipotence, His omniscience—
His divine attributes—and took on Himself the form of a
man with all the limitations that human nature has. He
humbly became obedient to God the Father. And then
He humbly took the role of Advocate (lawyer) for us.[4]
Each one agreed fully to His specific roll in order for us
to be brought back into right standing with God. I find
this awesome to think about: Each is equal in:

- holiness (without sin or evil)
- omnipresence (always present everywhere)
- omniscience (all knowing)
- omnipotence (all powerful)
- unity (one in purpose)

---

[1] Genesis 1:26
[2] John 1:1
[3] Philippians 2:6
[4] 1 John 2:1

- wholly committed (devoted to one another)

The Equality of the Godhead
In equality they are on the same level:

Father   -   Son   -   Holy Spirit

But in their function they are on different levels:

Father
      Son
            Holy Spirit

The equality of the Godhead does not change—only their function. They are ONE in agreement—even though their functions differ.

The Father sent the Son, Who sent the Holy Spirit.

- The **Father** is God – the **Final** Word
- The **Son** is God – the **Spoken** Word
- The **Holy Spirit** is God – the **Administrator** of the Word. He is the active Agent Who determines our individual assignments in life and empowers us to carry them out.

Each has His role and function. By comparing various Scriptures we can see the complementary roles they play:

"The Head of Christ is God."[5] Jesus became submissive to the Father when He came to live on this earth. He came to do the Father's will and to reveal the Father to us.

The Father honors the Son. *"And a voice from heaven said, "This is my Son, whom I love; with him I*

---

[5] 1 Corinthians 11:3

am well pleased."[6] *"Then the end will come, when [Jesus] hands over the kingdom to God the Father after he has destroyed all dominion, authority and power. For he must reign until he has put all his enemies under his feet. The last enemy to be destroyed is death. For he [the Father] 'has put everything under his [the Son's] feet.'"*[7]

The Son honors the Father. *"I honor my Father. I do only what the Father tells me to do."*[8] Why did Jesus get up early to pray to the Father? Why did He pray all night? To get instructions from the Father.

The Holy Spirit came to reveal Jesus to us and to give us power to live like Jesus. He speaks of Jesus, not of Himself. *"But when he, the Spirit of truth, comes, he will guide you into all truth. He will not speak on his own; he will speak only what he hears, and he will tell you what is yet to come. He will bring glory to me by taking from what is mine and making it known to you."*[9] The Holy Spirit makes Jesus real to us.

We Are Created in God's Image

How awesome it is to realize that we mere humans are created in His image. When God said that husband and wife would become one flesh, He meant for us to understand that the equality of a husband and wife is the same as in the Godhead.

"A man will leave his father and mother and be united to his wife, and they will become one flesh."[10] Not inferior or superior. We are one in equality, like the Father, Son and Holy Spirit.

---

[6] Matthew 6:17
[7] 1 Corinthians 15:24-26
[8] John 8:49
[9] John 16:13-14
[10] Genesis 2:24

"If we are children [of God], then we are heirs— heirs of God and co-heirs with Christ, if indeed we share in his sufferings in order that we may also share in his glory."[11] The King James Version says, *"we are joint-heirs."* The husband and wife share the same life in God: grace, adoption, authority, eternal life, etc.

Perhaps we can see it more clearly in chart form:

	God Head	**Husband-Wife**
In Their **Person**	Equality	Equality
In Their **Function**	Diversity	Diversity
In Final **Authority**	One Head—the Father	
	One Head—the Husband	

The importance of this biblical truth is more than merely gaining a comprehension of the concept. The whole idea of authority goes against our independent nature. We all would like to be able to do as the Old Testament Israelites did when, *"in those days...every man did that which was right in his own eyes."[12]* Of course the result of that was national sinfulness and chaos. As Bev mentioned when discussing the area of submission, it is not easy to yield to another's authority. Yet it is needed in the practical day-to-day living in our homes.

We see this clearly in family sit-coms on television. Dad is a wimp, mom mouths off to him, and they both give in to the whims of the children. The children are disrespectful to both parents and seem to make the decisions for the family. Because the scenes are intentionally wrapped in humor, we laugh. But deep down we know that something is wrong. What's wrong is that no one is in charge. Authority has been thrown

---

[11] Romans 8:17
[12] Judges 17:6

out the window. Anarchy reigns. Our children watch, and think this behavior is normal and is to be copied.

God is grieved that what He created—the family which He intended to represent Him and His love and care for us—would be distorted into a meaningless, chaotic, stressful environment in which to nurture the next generation.

In our Christian homes we can work out the area of authority by keeping in mind that God has declared us equal. We can accept our role in God's order for the home and learn to function in it, just as the members of the godhead function in their roles.

The Specific Roles Outlined in God's Word

• The Husband/Father - *"The husband is the head of the wife."*[13] – He is the final authority for his family:
• The Wife/Mother - *"As the church is subject unto Christ, so [let] the wives [be] to their own husbands."*[14]
• Children - *"Children obey your parents."*[15]
• All family members – *"Submit to one another out of reverence for Christ."*[16] *"Obey your leaders and submit to their authority. They keep watch over you as men who must give an account."*[17]

We men want our wives to be under our authority. Yet are we living properly under the authority of those whom God has placed over us, such as the government, our boss, and our spiritual leaders?

We see the importance of authority illustrated in the New Testament story of the Roman centurion, a military

---

[13] Ephesians 5:23
[14] Ephesians 5:24
[15] Ephesians 6:1 King James Version
[16] Ephesians 5:21
[17] Hebrews 13:17

leader.[18] His servant was gravely ill so he asked Jesus to heal him. When Jesus said, *"I will go and heal him,"* the centurion responded, *"Lord, I do not deserve to have you come under my roof. But just say the word, and my servant will be healed. For I myself am a man under authority, with soldiers under me. I tell this one, 'Go,' and he goes; and that one, 'Come,' and he comes. I say to my servant, 'Do this,' and he does it.' When Jesus heard this, he was astonished and said to those following him, 'I tell you the truth, I have not found anyone in Israel with such great faith.' Then he said to the man, 'Go! It will be done just as you believed it would.'"*

Jesus was astonished! This gentile understood what many of us as believers fail to grasp. In order to have authority, we must be under authority. Indeed, perhaps one of the reasons God established authority is to help us to see and evaluate how we respond to the authorities in our lives. God is looking at our attitude, to see if we are teachable.

- The husband fills the role or function of the head.
- The wife fills a supportive role.
- The children recognize and honor the leadership of their parents.

As we've seen, this does not mean the wife is inferior or less important, just that she has a different function. If she wants to know the full blessing of God in her life she can learn how to honor her husband as her head.

Submission to authority does not come easily, whether to the law of the land, to our teachers in a classroom setting, or to the family leader at home. Yet a significant thing happens when an individual is able to

---

[18] Matthew 8:5-13

visibly see the submission of his or her own authority to the one in authority over them.

Lead by Example

Husbands and fathers are to lead by example, not by might.

- *"I say to you, from now on, you shall not see Me until you say, 'Blessed is He who comes in the name of the Lord.'"*[19]

- *"Obey your leaders, and submit to them; for they keep watch over your souls, as those who will give an account. Let them do this with joy and not with grief, for this would be unprofitable to you."*[20]

- *"Appreciate those who diligently labor among you, and have charge over you in the Lord and give you instruction and esteem them very highly in love because of their work."*[21]

- *"You younger men, likewise be subject to your elders."*[22]

- *"Let every person be in subjection to the governing authorities. For there is not authority except from God, and those which exist are established by God."*[23]

- *"Do not sharply rebuke an older man, but rather appeal to him as a father, to the younger men as brothers."*[24]

Can a Wife Have Authority?

Of course she can. Let's hear from Bev now.

---

[19] Matthew 23:39
[20] Hebrews 13:17
[21] 1 Thessalonians 5:12-13
[22] 1 Peter 5:5
[23] Romans 13:1
[24] 1 Timothy 5:1

A wife has the authority of the various roles she plays in life. As a homemaker, she makes most of the household decisions. As a mother, she has authority over her children. On her job, she has the authority of whatever her position affords her. Usually, problems arise when a woman wants to usurp authority over her husband. Maybe he has abdicated his role as head of the home. Or maybe she perceives herself as more intelligent or more gifted than her husband. Sometimes she sees herself as more spiritual than he.

When a woman wants authority, including spiritual leadership, she may think that because she is equal to her husband, and perhaps brighter or more spiritually attuned, that she can take the headship over him. She may believe that submitting to him would hold her back from fulfillment.

Biblical Submission Frees a Woman to Be All God Wants Her to Be

In reality, by submitting to her husband in every way a woman will be set free to become all she is capable of and all she was meant to be.

A woman's value is equal to her husband's, but her role in their relationship is established in Ephesians 5:23: he is her head—her priest. As she elevates, honors, and respects him—in their relationship, before their family, before the world—she releases a spiritual blessing upon herself, her family, and her ministry.

In my ministry role as a Bible teacher, writer, and trainer of writers I have traveled outside my own country—both with Pete and alone. I've ministered in Switzerland, Brazil, and New Zealand—without Pete. My trips were not in defiance of him, but rather with his blessing—figuratively and literally. He doesn't feel threatened when I'm the one in front of an audience, in fact, he's my biggest fan.

We have a dear friend, a woman, who serves in an unusual role. She is the pastor of a local church. Her husband holds a secular job and has no desire or calling to be *in the ministry*. From what we can see, Kristeen is a woman with great spiritual depth, authority, and humility. Yet in their marriage and in their home, Kristeen is submitted to Wade. She respects and honors him as the head of their home.

If Kristeen failed to recognize and live under his authority, not only would her family and the congregation lose respect for both of them, the powers of Satan would have access to her and God would be limited in His blessing and fulfillment in her life, her family, and the church she leads.[25]

Authority is a God-given gift. It is not something that is merely learned from the scripture and the pulpit. It is learned by watching others live it out in practical ways, not only as people with different roles, but as people who are different from one another.

---

[25] 1 Corinthians 11:10 Amplified Bible

Chapter Ten

Differences by God's Design

Those who study marriage and the difficulties within marriages tell us that 75% of marriage problems have to do with the differences between men and women. Why is it then that we expect our spouse to think or act just like we do?

My Way Is the Right Way

We view our own way as the right way; any other way then, must be wrong, or at least not as good. Or perhaps we think of ourself as the one with the flaws or weaknesses and try to hide them. Why? God made us with our weaknesses. We need to learn to be thankful for them. Paul wrote, "When *I am weak, he is strong.*"[1] Then, *"We are weak in him, yet by God's power we will live."*[2]

As we each set out to improve our marriages, let's look at the ways God made us different. Keep in mind that these differences are by God's design and selection. It's not a matter of inferior and superior, but characteristics intentionally built in by God for the

---

[1] 2 Corinthians 12:10
[2] 2 Corinthians 13:4

functioning of the family. Whenever we step outside of our God-given design we weaken our marriage.

That's not to say we can't assist each other in our roles. God has given these differences to complete each other, not to compete with one another. God said, "*It is not good for the man to be alone. I will make a helper suitable for him.*"[3] A man needs a woman to be complete. The word in the King James Version is *helpmeet* meaning "exact complement." When we see the combination of love, balance and unity in a man and his wife, we see completion.

Remember, we married him or her for their strengths, and go home and live with their weaknesses. The very things that attracted us to one another can become the sources of greatest friction between us.

How Did God Design Us?

The story is in the first two chapters of Genesis. We overhear the Father, the Son, and the Holy Spirit talking, "*Let us make man in our image, in our likeness, and let them rule...God created man in his own image, in the image of God he created him; male and female he created them. God blessed them and said to them, 'Be fruitful and increase in number; fill the earth and subdue it.'*"[4] What a beautiful picture of how God intends for man and woman to function together.

When Adam saw Eve for the first time he didn't reject her. If he had, he would have been rejecting himself.

In counseling with married couples we often hear expressed, "I just don't know what to do." Yet most problems in marriages come—not from ignorance—but from unwillingness to do the right thing, choosing not to

[3] Genesis 2:18
[4] Genesis 1:26-28

follow, defying, or neglecting God's design and role for men and women. When we function in God's design and intent—His purpose and plan—we find fulfillment. A husband who makes decisions without the input of his wife's perspective has a narrow view of a situation. A wife who disregards her husband's wishes is missing a God-given element of completion for her life.

When a woman says her marriage vows, she lays her life on the line; traditionally even giving up her name. If the man doesn't pick up the leadership and responsibilities of the home, in time she will get frustrated and pick up that leadership.

Historically, a man was drawn to a woman and moved aggressively. She responded submissively. In many situations today these roles have been reversed. Yet completing one another is becoming one.

The Bible tells us to leave and cleave. *"A man shall leave his father and his mother and shall become united and cleave to his wife, and they shall become one flesh."*[5] The man and woman together are to reflect the image of God.

Relationship... love... balance... unity... all these are symbolic of the Godhead: the Father, the Son and the Holy Spirit. Remember, the Scriptures teach that the relationship between husband and wife are to reflect the Godhead itself. When we see that relationship of love, balance and unity in a man and his wife, we see completion.

Why is it that our differences are so readily the things that seem to drive us apart? Perhaps this poem says it best:

> If I do not want what you want; please try not to tell me that my want is wrong.

---

[5] Genesis 2:24 Amplified Version

Or if I believe other than you, at least pause before you correct my view.

Or if my emotion is less than yours, or more, given the same circumstances, try not to ask me to feel more strongly or weakly.

Or yet, if I act or fail to act, in the manner of your design for action, let me be.

I do not, for the moment at least, ask you to understand me. That will come only when you are willing to give up changing me into a copy of you.

I may be your spouse, your parent, your offspring, your friend, or your colleague. If you will allow me any of my own wants, or emotions, or beliefs, or actions, then you open yourself, so that some day these ways of mine might not seem so wrong, and might finally appear to you as right—for me.

To put up with me is the first step to understanding me. Not that you embrace my ways as right for you, but that you are no longer irritated or disappointed with me for my seeming waywardness. And in understanding me you might come to prize my differences from you, and, far from seeking to change me, preserve and even nurture those differences.[6]

I (Bev) love watching television shows that chronicle the lives of children born in multiples, whether twins or even sextuplets. Those known as "The Six-Pack," Ian, Adrian, Julian, Claire, Brenna and Quinn Dilley of Decatur, Indiana, are America's first-ever surviving sextuplets. Since their 1993 birth, television cameras have captured the major events in the children's lives. Although these six children share the same genetic

---

[6] *Different Drummers*, excerpted from *Please Understand Me*, 1998 by David Keirsey

makeup and have been reared in the same home, during the same time period, each is quite different from his siblings. Their parents Becki and Keith Dilley, readily reference the children's differences: Ian is a loner, Adrian is a risk taker, Claire is considered the boss and leader, Brenna is compassionate and quiet, Julian likes to go off and do his own things, and Quinn is the conscience of the group. One of the amazing things is that these characteristics were evident at an early age.

Should we be surprised that our husband or wife, born to a different family from our own, likely reared in a different town, perhaps during a slightly different time period and possibly in a different culture or sub-culture, will be more different than like us?

In our marriage seminars we ask our audience members which of them is in a marriage where one is a night owl married to an early bird; or where one prefers to arrive early and their spouse is habitually late; or is a social butterfly married to a loner; one wants to sleep with the window open and the other wants the room warm and cozy. It seems that almost everyone raises their hand with each question.

This is because opposites attract. We tend to marry someone different from us. We sense a lack in our own life and subconsciously look for someone that can balance us out. Then we proceed to try to change that person to become more like ourself.

Different by God's Design
Our differences are by God's design and selection. As we saw in Chapter Nine, it's not a matter of inferior and superior. Our value as men and women is equal. For the functioning of the family, our basic gender differences are built in by God for the enrichment of life, for the good of the community.

In God's infinite wisdom He planned that each child would have a father and a mother, thus providing the child a masculine and a feminine viewpoint: the tender, gentleness of a mother, and the strong, firm guidance of a father. But this duet is not only for the children's sake. God has given these differences for the health of the marriage as well. A husband and wife are not to compete with one another, but to complete each other. God said, *'It is not good for the man to be alone.'* [7] *'These two shall become one flesh.'* [8] Man needs a woman to be complete and a woman needs a man to be complete.[9]

Before we look at some of the ways God made us different, I want to remind us that these are generalizations. Which and how much are God-given, we can't discern.

• Men's blood is thicker and heavier than women's, with 20% more blood corpuscles, providing more oxygen to their bodies. Men have a higher ratio of muscle to fat—40% of their body is muscle. This makes it is easier for them to lose weight. Women's bodies consist of only 20% muscle, so it is harder for women to lose weight.

• Pound for pound a man is twice as strong as a woman. According to the U.S. Army, cardio-respiratory fitness in women on average is about 70% that of men. Muscular strength in women is about 65% that of men. The incidence of lower extremity injury in women in the military is approximately twice that of men primarily due to low muscular strength.[10] Women are

---

[7] Genesis 2:18

[8] Genesis 2:24 KJV

[9] Of course God can give complete contentment and fulfillment to those who remain single.

[10] *Concerns for Women Soldiers,*
http://www.usariem.army.mil/swasia/womencon.htm

constitutionally stronger than men—they live longer and are more resilient against fatigue, illness, famine, childbirth (!), and so forth.

• The skin of a man is thicker, less vulnerable to outside injury. As a result, he doesn't wrinkle as readily as a woman.

• Men have larger bones, and they are arranged differently.

• A woman's pubic bones are wider, requiring more energy to be put into each step, so she tires more easily.

Child psychologist Dr. James Dobson relates a humorous story about men and women in his best-seller, *Straight Talk to Men and Their Wives.* Several years ago a drug company conducted an experiment with all of the women in a small fishing village in South America. The women were all given an experimental birth control pill. They were given the same pill on the same date, and the prescription was terminated after three weeks to permit menstruation. "That meant, of course," Dr. Dobson says, "that every adult female in the community was experiencing premenstrual tension at the same time. The men couldn't take it. They all headed for their boats each month and remained at sea until the crisis had passed at home. They knew, even if some people didn't, that females are different from males...especially every twenty-eight days."[11]

• Men are competitors and conquerors; women are contributors and supporters. Men want to be in control. They are competition oriented. They usually have few good friends, probably because subconsciously they view every man as a competitor. This destroys friendships. That's why sports are so important to men.

---

[11] *Straight Talk to Men and Their Wives,* Dr. James Dobson, Word Publishing, Dallas, Texas, 1991, p. 181.

Even team sports have this element. A man is a winner because his team is a winner. When a couple takes a trip together they see the trip through different eyes. The woman views the trip as a time to contribute to one another. The man sees the trip as something to conquer. He's going to drive 500 miles (or kilometers) today if it kills him. This is also why he gets irritated with bathroom stops. He has miles to conquer. He's got to get there. A man is concerned with getting from A to B. The woman is concerned with what happens from A to B.

We need both of these characteristics, competetiveness and nurturing, for the survival of mankind. This can lead to real problems though. The man sees a girl he likes. He pursues her and convinces her to marry him. He has conquered. But once the relationship is established, his attitude is: "Ok, I've got the girl!" and he goes on to other things. Instead of immersing himself in the relationship, he pulls back. This creates deep insecurity in his bride. As he pulls back, she pursues and pressures him for more involvement. He pulls back further. Their love begins to die. God said he should put his wife on a pedestal, so to speak. Not to worship her, but to cherish and protect her. The wise bride will not pressure her reluctant husband. She will back off slightly, then he'll come back to her.

• From early childhood a boy wants to be the best. He sees every other boy as someone to compete with. He must be stronger, louder, faster, or smarter. Groups of boys quickly establish a pecking order. For a boy it's a contest until he figures out what social slot he fits into. Someone will surface as the leader, most want it to be himself. Girls see other girls as companions, friends, and team members. Their groups generally don't need a leader. If one emerges it's usually because others recognize her leadership skills and subconsciously

94

choose to let her lead. God made us with these differences.

• Women are relational creatures. They can weep when watching a TV show. The man may ask, "Why are you crying?" She could answer, "For the same reason you scream and yell over a touchdown made by a man you've never met." If we were to show photos of people's faces with various emotional expressions to a woman, she'll correctly identify the feelings. If she listens to taped conversations with the words garbled so she cannot understand them, she is twice as likely as a man to correctly identify the emotional content.

• Men are object oriented and women are relationship oriented. Watch a group of preschoolers. The boys are playing with toy cars and trucks, hammers and back-hoes. The noises they make mimic the sounds of the toys they hold. The girls are making just as much noise, but listen closely and you'll notice their sounds are words. They are talking to one another or talking to a doll. Maybe they're talking to no one in particular. This can be seen very early. A baby girl smiles more than a baby boy. She's more responsive to the cries of other babies in the hospital nursery than boy babies.

• A woman can give emotionally, and give, and keep on giving—until empty. Then she becomes bitter. Once bitter, there's too much distance between the two. If they don't divorce, they might merely become roommates—trying to stay out of each other's way.

• When problems arise, men instinctively look for someone else to blame. Women instinctively look to *themselves* and blame themselves. Men are hard on *others* instinctively. Women are hard on *themselves* instinctively.

- Women's emotions are generally closer to the surface than men's. "That men do not emote pain, hurt, and despair like women do seems to mean to some women that men are not feeling anything. The truth is men suck it up and just try to get along in life in general and with [women] in particular. Women should not measure or interpret a man's heart, soul, intent, or feelings based upon their own reactions. Women cry and talk; men don't ruminate on feelings, they try to do something about the situation. I guess that makes men lousy "girlfriends," but very helpful "partners" if women would respect their uniqueness."[12]

- A woman may not want a solution, but only to communicate with her husband. She may even resent his effort to solve what she views as only something she shared in conversation. However, God made men to be problem solvers. "His high levels of testosterone and vasopressin lead him toward problem-solving responses to stressors. So a man's brain and hormones compel him to respond to emotions and stress by either doing something or fixing something."[13] "Because he's supposed to just be a listening board (like a girlfriend or shrink?) and not help solve, repair, or attack her enemies, he is quiet. Why? Because he's failed, in his eyes, to be a man, her man. He's worthless, impotent to help her, to stop her pain. One man wrote, 'I've been relegated to being the warm, soft, cuddly teddy bear on her bed, instead of the white knight in her bed. I don't feel like a man. My self-esteem is in the bottom of the

---

[12] *The Proper Care and Feeding of Husbands*, by Dr. Laura Schlessinger, Harper Collins Publishers, 2004.
[13] Taken from *His Brain, Her Brain* by Walt Larimore, M.D. Copyright ©1988 by Zondervan. Used by permission of Zondervan.

well. I just want to be a man with the woman I love in my arms.'"[14]

Keep in mind that in God's wisdom He determined that each of us needs both a masculine and a feminine perspective on things: a male and female way of seeing things.

God Made These Differences in Men and Women

These differences between the sexes begin in the brain. Think of the meat of a walnut with its two halves. Each half is distinct, but connected to the other half. An eight-week-old fetus's brain looks much like a walnut and is about that size

Until the eighth week of gestation every human fetal brain looks female. The brain, like the rest of his body, becomes male as a result of two surges of the hormone testosterone—one during his eighth week of *life*, and one shortly after birth. Without this flooding of testosterone, a girl will result. She will have millions and millions of connections between the two halves of her brain.

This flooding of hormones creates an organ, the human brain, that generates typically boyish behavior such as rough-and-tumble play. Scientists call that moment of flooding *a glorious moment.*

After the flooding, the baby boy's two brain-halves will have much fewer connections—still millions, but significantly fewer. Behavioral differences appear early. For example, a one-day-old girl will look for longer periods at a face than at a mechanical mobile; a boy will prefer the mobile. Within a year of birth, boys and girls also prefer different toys. Boys prefer cars, trucks, balls

---

[14] *The Proper Care and Feeding of Husbands*, by Dr. Laura Schlessinger, Harper Collins Publishers, 2004.

and guns. Girls prefer dolls and tea sets. This causes the boys and girls—and later when they are men and women—to think differently from one another.

The main connection between the two hemispheres of the brain is known as the *corpus callosum* and is made of white matter. It is proportionately smaller in men than women. This may explain why men use only one side of the brain to process some problems for which women employ both sides. One could say that men are mono-minded and women are stereo-minded.

These differences in structure and wiring do not appear to have any influence on intelligence as measured by Intelligence (IQ) tests. It does seem, however, that the sexes carry out these tests in different ways. In one example, where men and women perform equally well in a test that asks them to work out whether nonsense words rhyme, brain scanning shows that women use areas on both the right and the left sides of the brain to accomplish the task. Men, by contrast, use only areas on the left side.

Because of the structure of his brain, when a man thinks of a problem or focuses on a concept he is able to tune out all else. He can compartmentalize his thoughts. With her extra brain connections, a woman can focus on one thing yet be aware of other things around her, and also of the past and the future. She can be preparing dinner, helping one child with her homework, chatting with someone on the telephone, and comforting a child with a wounded knee, all at once. Perhaps this is why as children we thought our mothers had eyes in the back of their heads.

By contrast, a man is able to mentally isolate his focus. He can sit in a noisy airport terminal, ignore the nearby passengers, the screaming children, the suitcases being wheeled over his toes, and the announcements on the loud speaker. He can tune everything out and be totally absorbed in a game on his handheld device.

Of course this is dealing only in generalities and there are degrees of differences within these generalities. Some women are more competitive than some men are; and some men are more relationally oriented than some women are.

We mentioned earlier the changes in our culture in recent decades and how it has affected the way men and women view themselves and one another. In times past, a woman could ask her mother or sisters to watch the children a while so she could get away. We now have isolated women who can never get away from their responsibilities. Many young wives today complain that it's easy for their husbands to take a day away from responsibilities, but they themselves never are relieved from their responsibilities. A wife may be a stay-at-home mom. When her husband comes home from work he expects his wife to protect his hours at home, letting him rest or recreate as he chooses.

More commonly she holds a job outside the home and comes home tired as well. But she has children to tend, meals to prepare, and housework to take care of. It's easy for either of these wives to feel resentful that her husband can relax at home while she is still on call even when she's asleep.

Without her mom or sisters nearby to relieve her, a woman needs her husband to guard such a time for her. We recommend she have several hours to herself at least once a week.

Even when a woman has lost sleep because of caring for a sick child, some husbands will say, "Sure honey, you sleep in, I'll watch the kids." But when she gets up an hour or two later than usual, she might find the children have neither been fed nor changed out of their wet diapers. Most men are not intentionally selfish in this regard. They merely fail to see the need to relieve their wife from *all* responsibility now and then. They are simply unaware!

What can a woman do? It's up to her to gently educate him. She need not lecture or whine. She can humbly let him know what she needs. She can say, "Yes, I'll appreciate a chance to catch up on that lost sleep. And will you see that the children are fed and changed too?"

This does not deviate from the pattern God gave of Christ and the church. In fact, Jesus specifically told His disciples that they should ask for their needs to be met.[15] This is consistent with the pattern we see in the Old Testament: God has always wanted His people to share with Him what they need.[16]

Non-Gender Differences in Individuals

Not all differences in a marriage are related to gender. Each individual differs from others in a variety of ways. One of those is in the way we feel and think about things. We thoughtlessly expect others to feel the way we do in a given situation; or we expect them to process thoughts and come to the same conclusions given the same information. This lack of empathy—understanding and entering into another's feelings—is what makes thoughtlessness possible and results in hurt feelings. We don't realize the effect we have on others, even our spouse. According to Harley Willard, in some families, "*an angry outburst* is regarded by some as a creative expression. *Disrespect* is viewed as helping the other spouse gain proper perspective. And *a demand* is nothing more than encouraging a spouse to do what he

---

[15] Matthew 7:7; 21:22; John 11:22; 14:13-14; 15:7, 16; 16:22-26
[16] Psalm 50:15; 55:16; 91:15

or she should have done all along. None of these is seen as one spouse gaining at the other's expense, because the spouse who is inflicting the pain does not feel the pain."[17] [*Emphasis mine*]

I deal at length with non-gender differences in *God's Gift of Friendship - Tools for Improving Relationships*.[18] I'll only mention them briefly here.

- **Instincts** – the abilities with which we were born such as blinking, or the reaction to surprise.
- **Habits** – behavior developed by repeating an action.
- **Culture** – elements of society learned from those around us.
- **Genetics** – characteristics we inherit from our parents.
- **Value System** – that to which we attach worth or value.
- **Personality Types** – formed by a combination of genetics, environmental influence, cultural settings, and our in-born temperament.
- **Love Languages** – We each have a primary way we like to receive love: Encouraging Words; Acts of Service; Gift Giving; Quality Time; and Physical Touch and Closeness.[19]
- **Spiritual Gifts** – Three lists are found in scripture: The Motivational Gifts found in Romans 12:6-8; The Manifestation Gifts found in 1 Corinthians 12:7-11; and The Office Gifts found in Ephesians 4:11-12.

---

[17] *Love Busters: Overcoming Habits That Destroy Romantic Love*, by Harley Willard F. Jr., Fleming Revell, 1972
[18] *God's Gift of Friendship – Tools for Improving Relationships*, by Beverly Caruso, available from www.PeteandBevCaruso.com.
[19] For an in depth study of Love Languages, see *The Language of Love*, by Gary Smalley, John Trent.

There are multiple systems in the human body with seemingly opposing purposes: the circulatory; digestive; nervous; respiratory, etc. We can see this for example in the arm. With one set of muscles we can push, with another we pull. Yet God designed us so that by working together these systems make the body whole. Just as the human body ministers to itself, so it is in our relationships.

Often misunderstandings arise because we do not see that our cultures, instincts, habits, giftings, and other differences cause others to view life from a perspective different from our own. If we want our marriage to be strong, we can strive to gain an understanding of our own gifts as well as those of our spouse. We can strive to accept their differences so that we can fulfill the prayer of Jesus in John 17, that His followers would be in such unity that the world will know that we are one.[20]

Recognizing differences is only one of the first steps toward healthy relationships. Equally important is learning communication skills. Few of us know instinctively how to communicate effectively. But we can develop skills so that we can intentionally keep the lines of communication open in our most cherished relationships.

---

[20] See John 17:21

Chapter Eleven

Intentional Communication, Key to Marital Harmony

A heavy wooden plaque hung above the pastor's desk making it hard to focus on the matter at hand. It wasn't the wood, or even the letters themselves so carefully carved into the surface. It was the words: *Communication is Equal to Calvary.* The words rang in my (Pete's) ears for many days. At first they troubled me. *How could anything come close to the value of the cross?*

At last the meaning became clear. The passage in Romans made the statement, *"How shall they believe in him of whom they have not heard?"*[1] Without someone taking the time to tell us about the cross—communicating—the cross has no effect on our lives. Communication is the key.

Much has been written about the differences in the ways men and women communicate. Little has been said about the many ways our communication is similar. In an analysis of over 1,200 research studies. only a 1% variance in communication behavior resulted from

---

[1] Romans 10:14

gender patterns.[2] The reality is that those differences cause much of the friction in most marriages. We may know better, but subconsciously we expect our spouse to think and feel in the same ways we do. So we mindlessly divulge our thoughts as they come, or we hold them inside, expecting the other to know what we're thinking.

Many people perceive a difference in communication style as the other party's personal failing. If we could see style differences for what they are, merely different from our own, then a lot of blaming and negative feelings could be eliminated. Nothing hurts more than being told our intentions are bad when we know they're good, or being told we're doing something wrong when we know we're just doing it our way.

In our book, *God's Gift of Friendship - Tools for Improving Relationships,* we covered communication quite thoroughly.[3] That is, communication in general. Rather than covering ground already covered there, let's take a quick overview of those principles, then we'll look at specific communication issues within marriage.

Overview of General Communication Principles
- Make time for communication. By scheduling our *marriage* first on our calendars we can prevent life from squeezing out our top priority.
- Our words are powerful. They have the ability to cause deep emotional hurt, or they can bring comfort and healing to another.

---

[2] From an online course of study, *Interpersonal Relationships,* Chapter five,
http://members.tripod.com/nwacc_communication/index.htm, A Communication site for students and teachers, by Lynn Meade.
[3] *God's Gift of Friendship - Tools for Improving Relationships*, by Beverly Caruso, available from www.PeteandBevCaruso.com.

- There are several levels of communication from the *Clichés* that we use with strangers ("Good morning. How are you?"), through the *Fact Level* (sharing what we know), the *Emotional Level* (sharing what we feel), to *Transparency* with our closest friends (being known for who and what we really are). Within marriage, we can reach a deeper level still, that of *Intimacy*.
- We generally put most of our thoughts into our words. Yet words make up only 7% of spoken communication. Our tone of voice comprises another 38%. Few of us consciously think about the other 55%—non-verbal communication, mostly body language.
- We can learn to avoid common hindrances to good communication:
    - Fear of being known for who we really are
    - Failure to use feedback
    - The tendency to protect what we perceive as our rights
    - Neglecting the important role of being a good listener
    - The mistaken idea that we must agree on every point
    - Viewing communication as a win-lose battle, rather than choosing to agree to disagree
    - Speaking in an accusatory way rather than expressing our feelings in a neutral way such as, "I feel lonely," or "I feel the need for..." By using "I feel" we free the other person to either try to meet our need, or to acknowledge it without feeling judged.
    - Neglecting the most valuable aid for good communication—prayer

Male-Female Communication Differences

105

Keeping It Fresh

Let's start our examination of male-female communication styles by discrediting a long-held belief: *Women talk more than men.* Recent research has shown "some intriguing differences: women are more talkative than men when conversing with children and college classmates, while men are more talkative than women with spouses and strangers. With strangers, women try to form a connection, while men seek to influence the listener." [4] The report went on to say, "These findings compellingly debunk simplistic stereotypes about gender differences in language use.... The notion that the female brain is built to systematically out-talk men is hard to square with the finding that gender differences appear and disappear, depending on the interaction context."

The Importance of Openness and Honesty

Dr. Willard Harley writes: "To help remind couples how important honesty is in marriage, I have written the *Policy of Radical Honesty*: Reveal to your spouse as much information about yourself as you know; your thoughts, feelings, habits, likes, dislikes, personal history, daily activities, and plans for the future." He goes on to say, "Self-imposed honesty with your spouse is essential to your marriage's safety and success. Honesty will not only bring you closer to each other emotionally, it will also prevent the creation of destructive habits that are kept secret from your partner."[5]

---

[4] *It's Official: Men Talk More Than Women*, by Brandon Keim, November 09, 2007, issue of Parade Magazine. The study was originally published in *Personality and Social Psychology Review*.
[5] A Summary of Dr. Harley's Basic Concepts, Willard F. Harley, Jr., Ph.D., author of *His Needs, Her Needs, Building an Affair-proof Marriage*, Fleming Revell.

Indicate When Something is Especially Significant

Men tend to get used to hearing their wife's voice and not be aware when she is relating something she cares deeply about. A wise woman will 'communicate the serious things in a special way so the husband will pay particular attention and not consider it just an ordinary run-of-the-mill conversation. We can do something different like hold his hand and say, 'We need to discuss something important to me.'"[6]

Time for Communication

We each need to make time to communicate; it doesn't just happen. If we don't, our relationships can easily drift apart. By making a conscious effort to plan time for communication, we tell the other person that he or she is important to us.

Make your highest priority to take time alone with each other, so it will never be replaced by activities of lesser value. Your career, your time with your children, maintenance of your home, and a host of other demands will all compete for your time together. [7]

Pete and I have found that by making time together a priority we can keep our communication channels open. Because we work together as partners we no longer need to schedule time for communication. But when the children were young and our schedules frequently took us in opposite directions, it was necessary to consciously choose and plan to take time together just to fill one another in on both our activities and our thoughts. Most couples must make a conscious effort to share with one

---

[6] *The Proper Care and Feeding of Husbands*, by Dr. Laura Schlessinger, Harper Collins Publishers, 2004.
[7] Summary of Basic Concepts for Marriage, Dr. Willard E. Harley, Jr., PhD, author of *His Needs, Her Needs: Building an Affair-proof Marriage*.

another. We recommend a minimum of one hour once a week. Ideally it will be more like thirty minutes every day.

The timing of such communication is important. Women are ready to jump in immediately. Our daughter learned quickly in her marriage that after a day of hard work and a long commute, her husband needed about thirty minutes of down time before hearing about her day, or being expected to interact with the family. After unwinding he's ready to relate.

Be Alert to Signs of Closure

Sometimes we sense our spouse has closed him or herself off from us. The symptoms are many. Just a portion of a list from Gary Smalley: [8]

- Unjust criticism
- Harsh words
- Communicating that the other's opinions don't matter
- Joking about one's character or physical flaw
- Sarcastic statements
- Forcing what doesn't seem right
- Refusing to admit when he or she is wrong

Gary calls this a "closed spirit." He points out a number of steps toward opening that spirit. Among them:

- Demonstrate tenderheartedness.
- Listen carefully to what is said and how it is said.
- Touch the other person gently.
- We'll deal with his last point in a later chapter: Ask for forgiveness.

---

[8] Gary Smalley, the video series, *Hidden Keys to Loving Relationships*.

Frustration Tolerance Levels

Two couples who were close friends had spent the evening together. A sensitive subject came up that needed to be discussed. One of the husbands abruptly left the room and closed himself in the bathroom. His wife immediately broke into tears. "He always does this when this subject comes up." In fact, she told her friends, there were a number of subjects that her husband refused to talk about at all. Instead, he always walked out on the conversation.

What this man was reacting to has been called the Frustration Tolerance Level. When some people feel a certain emotion begin they refuse to allow those feelings to surface. Perhaps they're at the point of losing their temper, or they feel they might cry in front of others, or a subject is extremely painful to deal with, or they aren't willing to bear the truth about themselves. Instead, they close themselves off lest their undesirable emotions get exposed.

This may seem to be the best way to handle strong emotions. After all, who wants to deal with an angry man or a crying woman, or vice versa? This, however, leaves the other party or parties hanging with an unresolved issue. Some things *must* be discussed.

How can we deal with our Frustration Tolerance Level? If we recognize that when a certain subject comes up, or that when we have an emotional response we don't want to express, we can acknowledge that we have reached our Frustration Tolerance Level. We can acknowledge that it is a problem we need to deal with for the sake of our relationships.

Then we can consciously and earnestly ask the Lord to help us. It might be that the Holy Spirit will reveal to us the origin. He may give us insight into the reason for the problem. It might be that we will have to press past the intense emotion, such as to allow ourself to cry, or to display controlled anger. Repentance may be needed if there is an element of sin involved. We probably will need to ask for forgiveness from those close to us for closing them off in the past.

Those who are dealing with people with a low Frustration Tolerance Level may have to lay a ground work of prayer in order to help the family member or friend to acknowledge and deal with their closed spirit. It is well worth the prayer and the patience required in order to see them set free of this harmful pattern.

Issues of Control within Marriage

Both men and women are prone to use techniques to control the marriage. We may not be consciously aware that's what we're doing. When a woman withholds herself from lovemaking unless her husband meets her expectations, she is manipulating him. Some would say she is prostituting herself—giving herself only in exchange for something she wants. Conversely when a man withholds affection except when his wife is doing things the way he wants them, she feels used and deprived. Control can be manifested in finances, or by refusing to talk, or talking too much or disrespectfully, by withholding affection, and in numerous other ways. Regardless of the method, the message is the same: I value my desires and needs more than I value you and your desires and your needs.

As we saw in Ephesians 5:21, we are to submit to one another—one of the truest expressions of respect and love.

Rabbi Abraham J. Twerski offers some helpful advice[9] for avoiding the tendency to control:

---

[9] Rabbi Abraham J. Twerski, in *Control Issues in Marriage*, http://www.JewishWorldReview.com

• Stick to the issues! No name calling! Promise each other to stick to the issues and avoid any and every kind of personal attack.

• Don't make winning an argument an ego issue. Deal with the issues for what they are, and get your pride out of the way. "Incidentally," says the Rabbi, "one man told me what brought peace into their marriage. 'I didn't want to lose an argument,' he said. 'But then I realized that if I won, that meant that she lost. I didn't want to be married to a loser. So we stopped fighting about things and began discussing them on their merits.'"

• Make an agreement to negotiate and compromise. Marriage should not be seen as a struggle to see who will win.

• If things do not seem to be working out well, *seek competent counseling.* Find a counselor with established competence in marriage problems. It is not necessary for both partners to go. Seek guidance for yourself. Our best intentions for coping with a controlling person may backfire. Expert advice is invaluable.

• Remember Solomon's wise words. *"The way of a fool is straight in his own eyes, but he who listens to advice is wise"*[10] There are many reasons we may not be able to see a situation correctly, and we may react in a counterproductive manner. A wise person seeks counsel. Be wise!

Listening with Our Heart

What the person desires to communicate is far more important than how it is delivered. When I (Bev) began my writing career in my forties, I discovered that I hear things with the ear of an editor—and most people don't. I had always wondered how others could overlook the

---

[10] Proverbs 12:15

incorrect grammar or awkward word selection of others. It was easy for me to miss what someone, whether a friend or the pastor or speaker, was saying because I got distracted by the misuse of words. This discovery has helped me to ignore the preciseness of how the message could have been delivered and to focus more on listening with my heart. It has been a process; I've made great strides in learning to listen more with my heart rather than my head.

Stick to the Issues

We tend to see links between any two subjects. What happened yesterday, last week or even five years ago, is related to the topic at hand. We must make a conscious effort to stick to the issues and avoid bringing into our conversations reminders of our spouse's failures, personal attacks, and anything else that is not directly a part of the matter being discussed. A wise partner will recognize this tendency and gently help the speaker to stick to the topic.

Agree to Disagree

In any relationship there will be at least two ways of viewing any subject. Nowhere will any of us ever find someone who agrees with us on everything. If we're truly communicating with one another, we will have times when we won't and can't reach agreement. Some couples try to take turns making the final decisions in such cases, only to discover that they can't agree on who had the last turn. Some techniques that have helped us to deal with this problem are quite simple. First, we have fundamentally agreed, whenever possible, to negotiate and compromise. We are aware that marriage should not be seen as a struggle to see who will win.

Research shows that "69% of conflicts are never resolved, even years later...people argue about the same stuff! You will always have a set of unresolved issues with whomever you marry!"[11] When we disagree with our spouse we can take an obstinate position such as: "Yes, dear, anything you say," or "No way am I going to agree with you on this." Or we can agree to disagree: "I can see some of your points have merit; they make sense. Some of it I just don't agree with. Let's talk about it." In those areas where we'll never agree, a couple can learn to cope with their differences by nurturing respect and acceptance of their spouse.

Helpful Communication Techniques and Tips
  We sometimes use a rating system to help us understand the strength of the other's emotional investment in an issue. Do we want to spend a free day together in the mountains, hiking and having lunch beside a stream? Or do we want to go to visit friends we haven't seen for a long time? Each of us will state the strength of our desire in terms of a number. A *one* (1) would mean that we don't want to do the activity. A *ten* (10) means that the desire to do it is very strong. It might look like this:
  Bev: Drive to the mountains = 8 Visit friends = 3
  Pete: Drive to the mountains = 5 Visit friends = 8
  Our totals are: Mountains = 13   Friends = 11
  In this case we would spend the day in the mountains. We've found it is seldom necessary to actually do the math. Just expressing our desires in numbers usually makes it clear whose preference will be followed.
  Another technique is to list all the options of a matter as pro and con. We ask ourselves what are the good, or necessary, elements of an issue. Those elements are listed on one side of a paper. Then we list the negative elements in another column. By getting the options

---

[11] Dr. John Gottman, The Gottman Institute, Seattle, WA USA

visibly before us, it's easier to determine which way to decide.

The important thing about making decisions is for each to be open and non-judgmental of the other's feelings and statements. Of course this applies to all communication. We want to give our spouse the freedom to express him or herself freely and without ridicule or condemnation.

Some additional things to remember when communicating:[12]

- Don't hold back - express yourself
- Don't presume to judge
- Adopt a learner's attitude - listen with your heart
- Think before you speak
- Don't make the mistake of feeling you *must* win
- Focus on your own part of the blame
- Focus on the other person's viewpoint
- Accept differences of opinion
- Be concise
- Use feedback: parroting (repeating the details back to confirm clarity of understanding) and paraphrasing (putting into one's own words what they believe the speaker meant—especially regarding emotions).

What Constitutes a Good Fight?

Ideally a married couple will always get along, seeing eye-to-eye on every issue. You and I don't live in ideal marriages. No one does. There will be differences of opinion, different ways of viewing life. Should one party merely close *self* off and immerse him or herself into the

---

[12] For an expanded look at these elements of communication see *God's Gift of Friendship – Tools for Improving Relationships*, Chapter 8, available at: www.PeteandBevCaruso.com.

other? As I found, that's a path filled with frustration and folly.

There will be disagreements, sometimes strong ones, vocal ones. A husband might be sitting in the passenger seat while his wife drives: "For heaven's sake," he barks, "don't you know how to drive?" She might respond defensively with, "Stop telling me how to drive." She might pull over to the curb at the first opportunity, get out of the car and hand him the keys and calmly say, "Okay, you do the driving." For some couples this technique might work. For others it would be the beginning of a long, drawn out verbal battle or worse yet, a long silent trip.

A third response might be that she speaks gently and says something like, "I feel frustrated when you tell me how to drive. I try not to tell you how to drive. Please don't tell me how."

When a quarrel seems imminent we can follow these steps:

- Choose to remain calm, recognizing our own feelings
- Choose our words carefully, using non-defensive language
- Recall the value with which we hold our spouse and our marriage
- Intentionally validate our spouse

Letters to Our Spouse

Just as with words of affirmation, some of us find writing a note on a greeting card, or a letter expressing our feelings, far easier than it is for others. Yet seeing the feelings and thoughts of the one we love written in their hand or even printed out from their computer or in an email is a special experience.

As one married to a *non-natural-writer*, I cherish those rare visible expressions of Pete's love for me. He's penned loving notes, written sweet prose on greeting cards, and even attempted to write a love song. One of my most treasured gifts came as words he wrote on a recent birthday card. I've read them at least weekly for many months. Of course he never intended that anyone else would ever see them. With his permission I share them here:

--

December 8

My Dearest Darling,

I love you so much. I love you whether we are working out problems or talking about dreams.

The closeness we share never runs out and never will. We laugh, flirt, make out, pet, and drive each other crazy, but also keep each other sane.

We hold each other tight and we hold each other together. We melt each other and build each other up.

Your smile lifts my spirit. Your dancing eyes make me adore you. You are my perfect partner in every way.

It saddens me that others can't seem to find the kind of love we have.

One lifetime is not enough to show you how much I care for and love you and how much you mean to me.

Nothing could change How Much I Love You!!

Pete

To those who have never put their feelings for their spouse in writing: Give it a try! You'll bless her or his socks off. You may be surprised to find it one of their most valued treasures.

The Importance of Humor

I've always admired those who spontaneously bring humor into tense situations. There are families who know how to laugh together, to laugh at themselves, and just to laugh because it's fun. Such families tend to be healthier, both physically and emotionally, as well as relationally. Finding healthy humor in everyday life is a good way to let the tension out of otherwise stressful situations.

We're not talking about sarcastically pointing out one another's weaknesses or faults, in a teasing tone. That tends to leave a sting, if not a doubt about the teaser's love. We can say something we think is a tiny pebble. But to the brunt of the joke it was a heavy rock. Some folks fail to realize that others tend to feel things several levels deeper than they do.

We can keep in mind that we each tend to see situations through the lens of our background. For one who comes from a serious-prone family, arriving at a park only to learn the lunch is still sitting in the basket on the table at home would be seen as a tragedy. For his spouse from an easy-going household, the sight of the family gathered around an empty picnic table, wide-eyed with astonishment could trigger hilarious laughter. For either one, the remedy will be the same—replace or retrieve the lunch. It will simply be less stressful for those who can see the situation through a lens of humor.

Did you know that laughing...?
- Conditions our heart muscle
- Exercises our lungs and diaphragm
- Works all the abs and thoracic muscles
- Boosts the immune system
- Increases adrenaline and blood flow to the brain
- Lowers blood pressure

- Improves respiration

Plus, laughter lessens fear, anger, anxiety, physical pain, depression, and increases mental alertness, creativity, and memory. Wise is the one who brings humor into their marriage and into their life.

Code Word: Quiet!

Preston Cosgrove offers a helpful way of dealing with touchy issues. "When Jennifer and I got married, I was in graduate school and she was teaching middle school. She'd come home exhausted, yearning for peace and quiet. But a day of only books for company left me bubbling with enthusiastic chatter about things such as the Italian unification process. Partway through my debriefing, Jennifer would blurt out, "Be quiet! You're talking too much and I'm not interested in that stuff." Needless to say, she was feeling frustrated, and I was hurt.

"Then I had an inspiration—a code word. If my stories were dragging on, saying the code word would allow Jennifer to communicate in a gentler, less abrasive manner that she needed a break. Since to Jennifer my stories seemed endless and they'd definitely become divisive, I chose *Vietnam* as our word.

"Over dinner a few nights later, I was recounting innumerable details about American foreign policy when Jennifer sighed heavily, put down her fork, and looked at me. Seeing *Vietnam* on the tip of her tongue, I quickly stopped talking. After a few minutes we began to chat about the upcoming weekend. Success! Since that night our code word has given us many peaceful dinnertime conversations."[13]

---

[13] Preston Cosgrove, from *Marriage Partnership Magazine,* Thursday, November 01, 2007

Some prefer a physical signal, not just for talking too much. There are other areas when a person needs to let their spouse know what they're thinking—without using words. When in public, I've seen subtle signals and watched the response between couples. Sometimes it has been a discrete tapping of a finger on a watch face, followed a few minutes later by the spouse politely excusing the two from a social setting. I've watched someone pull on their earlobe and seen their spouse change the subject. It only takes creativity and commitment to be attentive to find ways to communicate with one another.

Prayer is Key to Good Communication

We've mentioned the need for prayer several times already. Let's take a closer look at it, for perhaps it is the most important, yet often missing, element in a marriage.

During the early years of our marriage we prayed together at the usual times: before meals and at bedtime. Of course these should not be disparaged, nor neglected. Yet we knew something was missing. In our fifteenth year together God sovereignly led us to begin reading the Bible and praying together each day, usually for two hours.

Our prayer time together has become an integral part of our marriage. Perhaps it is the main reason ours is a love that keeps on growing. In the next chapter we'll share some of our experiences in prayer, some results, and some prayer methods that we've learned along the way.

Keeping It Fresh

Chapter Twelve

The Couple That Prays Together Stays Together

When we learn that a certain couple doesn't pray together our hearts ache. *Our* prayer-time together is such a central part of our relationship that we can't imagine being without it.

You might remember that during our first time alone together—before we even began dating—we prayed together. In fact, God said to Pete then and there, "This is your wife." Wisely he didn't tell me about it for a long time.

During the months we were dating we ended each time we were together with prayer. What a restraining factor that was for us as our wedding date drew near! It also helped us lay the foundation for our relationship: Christ at the center of our lives and relationship. Even during our first fifteen years, before we began spending long seasons in prayer together, we occasionally enjoyed significant times together before the Lord.

A drastic change began during that fifteenth year when Pete invited a visiting missionary to speak at the church we were pastoring. After Ed brought a message from God's Word, his wife Ruth joined him. They moved among the congregation, praying for various needs. From my seat I could see the cleansing tears and the joy-filled smiles on the faces of those God touched that morning. It was an uplifting time for everyone.

After the service, we drove Ed and Ruth to a nearby restaurant for lunch. I remember thinking how beautifully this couple worked together—what great unity I sensed between them. And I recall the little twinge of longing I felt.

For years, I'd wanted to be an integral part of Pete's ministry—not just a background figure or a resource. Not that I didn't carry many responsibilities. But I wanted to be closer to Pete and his work. I wanted to be at his side, ministering to people with him. So far, it hadn't happened. I hoped that over lunch I could slip in some questions about the husband-wife relationship—gently, of course.

At the restaurant, our new friends told story after story of their work in Argentina. They spoke with such enthusiasm and brightness. At the central core of everything they shared was the warmth and closeness of their relationship.

I must admit, I was feeling a little envious when Pete surprised me with an abrupt declaration. In a moment's lull Pete said, "Ed, I'm jealous of the way your wife ministers with you."

Ed enthusiastically explained that he made Ruth's spirituality a priority. He said he knew how easy it was for a Christian man to be so caught up in his business, whatever it may be, that he unwittingly becomes neglectful of his spiritual responsibility to his wife. He said that he and Ruth made daily concerted prayer together a top priority. He finished with a strong pitch to Pete about putting a spiritual relationship with me at the top of his list, followed closely by the governing of our household.

I'm embarrassed to say that my inner response to what Ed said—especially the part about prayer together was—*that will be the day!*

Not that Pete was not a man of prayer. In Bible College he had started a daily 6 a.m. prayer meeting. Over the years, he'd met weekly with various other ministers for early morning prayer. Of course we had what I called our *goodnight prayer* together, a sort of wrap-up prayer for the day.

But what I longed for was a deep unity in prayer, a spiritual relationship in which we prayed in agreement about the common problems of life in our active household. I had tried to get Pete to pray like that with me for years with no success. Long ago, I'd given up trying.

After lunch, I wondered if Ed's suggestion about praying together made any impression on Pete. I certainly never guessed he had taken it as a mandate from God!

The next morning, Pete informed me that we were going to start praying together every day—starting right then. As we knelt together I was overwhelmed with his impassioned confession at having neglected the spiritual aspect of our relationship. The following Sunday, he continued to amaze me when he made this announcement to the congregation we were pastoring: "For years, I've made myself available to everyone else. My wife has even had to make appointments with me, just to talk about household needs. Now I see that Bev is my number one *sheep*. And I intend to minister to her needs first."

After telling the congregation he was making me his number one sheep, Pete assured them of our commitment to pray for them as well as ourselves. He even went so far as to tell them when our *protected time* of prayer was going to be, and asked that no one phone us during that time except in an emergency.

Anyone in ministry who might be reading these words, may feel as I felt, that Pete's bold statement would make some in the congregation feel neglected. Quite the opposite was true. As one woman told me, "Since part of your commitment was to pray together for us, it made us feel more secure."

Even for those who are not in positions of church leadership, the same need for spiritual unity applies. Pete and I discovered that for a husband and wife, a God-centered relationship must be a priority. Commitment is the key.

For us, the best time was first thing in the morning. We realize that this timing will not work for everyone, since the workday starts early for some and getting children up and off to school can also compete. The point is to do what works for the couple—and most of all to make the commitment. Setting a regular time, whenever it may be, will help to keep that commitment.

We urge husbands and wives who want to build this kind of spiritual fellowship into their marriage to find a format that works. A devotional book may be helpful, as long as it does not become an end in itself. We suggest simple, honest prayers. This may not be easy at first. But the rewards in renewed, open communication are wonderful.

We also recommend making a commitment to read the Scriptures together. It doesn't have to be a long passage. Taking turns reading short passages aloud might work. Soon most couples find themselves drawn into discussions about God's Word. This also makes it easier to think about a given passage all through the day.

As we think about a passage over and over, it gradually works its way into the center of our life.

Pete and I began praying together by taking turns. Soon we found that when one of us prayed about something, the other sometimes had knowledge or just a sense that God had already answered the prayer, or would have insight into the situation being prayed about. We would break into the other's prayer and share.

Gradually, we moved into a method of praying that has become almost a three-way conversation. If one of us is praying, the other is free to insert a brief comment, much the way we do in casual conversations with others. Sometimes the Lord brings things to our minds that lead us in an entirely different direction from the things we've set out to pray about.

The most important thing for me was the work that God was doing in Pete's life. He wants to share insights he has gained in the years since his understanding of spiritual headship became clearer:

Like most men, I suppose, I thought success had nothing to do with the home. A man's sense of self-worth generally comes from successes outside the home, mainly from his job. The world measures a man's success by whether he rises to the top in his field, by the amount of money he earns, and by the admiration he receives from numbers of people.

God created men with the desire to succeed and there is nothing wrong with these feelings. But unless a man is taught where true success lies, he has no understanding of his responsibilities first to God and, if he is married, at home. He thinks of his roles as husband and father primarily in terms of the paycheck he brings home. And his mind dwells on his job, quotas, deadlines and promotions.

Even we ministers tend to view our position in this light. Our work is the ministry. We counsel, teach, and meet people's needs. We tend to think we're successful if we can do these things well, if our congregation is growing, and if the church's programs are operating smoothly. As a result, we are just as likely as other men to neglect personal spiritual responsibilities and the needs of our families.

But the Bible measures success differently. The foundation of success has nothing to do with money, not even with family and friends. True achievement, by biblical standards, is found not so much in what we do as in who we are. The more we become like Jesus, the more truly successful we are. The deeper we develop our relationship with the Creator, the greater our spiritual prosperity.

The notions we have of success from a human point of view tend to focus away from the out workings of this relationship with God. The man who loves God will obviously be taken care of by Him. The man who communicates with God will understand how to manage his life wisely. The one who loves God will love others. It is easy to see why the only occurrence of the word *success* in the Bible describes the effects of obedience to the Word of God. *"This book of the law shall not depart out of thy mouth; but thou shalt meditate therein day and night, that thou mayest observe to do according to all that is written therein: for then thou shalt make thy way prosperous, and then thou shalt have good success."* [1] *[Emphasis mine]*

We too often accept the world's definition of success as our goal. I did the things that I thought would make me a success. I now see that they were things that satisfied my ego. I became a workaholic, though I didn't

---

[1] Joshua 1:8, King James Version

see it that way. I thought I was *sold out to God*. I didn't know how to take time to enjoy my children, and even felt guilty if I took a half-day off to visit my mother.

I also knew Bev had wanted me to pray regularly with her. But I couldn't see the importance of it, and I was blind to this need in her.

When Ed told me I should pray with Bev every day I received it as a charge from God. Gradually I was able to see that I had been thinking the way of the world, not God's way.

Through my prayer time with Bev I learned that God views the home as the smallest unit of the church. He places each married man in the office of husband, and He sees every man as a minister in his own home. For those of us called to leadership in the church, the Apostle Paul gave a prerequisite in the form of a question: *"How can a man who does not understand how to manage his own family have responsibility for the church of God?"*[2]

I also learned to better understand Bev through our prayer time. I realized that God created women to receive their sense of success and fulfillment in a far different way than men. A wife's desire is *"toward her husband.*[3]*"* I saw that Bev, like all other women, is happiest when she knows that her husband truly loves her and is committed to showing he cares for her.

Learning how to meet Bev's needs came through reading the Word and through my relationships with other Christian men. Primarily, of course, it came as she and I shared our lives at a deeper level in prayer.

---

[2] 1 Timothy 3:5, The Jerusalem Bible
[3] Genesis 3:16

The changes this made in our relationship are too great to tell, both in nature and in number. To mention only a few:

- We learned to work better as a team in our marriage, our parenting roles, and in ministry.
- Answers to prayer became regular and frequent.
- We both gained a new perspective of the other and the richness of their walk with God.
- Our prayers became less self-, family-, and pastoral-oriented and expanded to include extended family, others' ministries, and other spheres of society, such as: education; the media; entertainment; commerce; and government. As our prayer life together developed it expanded beyond our family and ministry to include others.

Bev shares this aspect of our prayer:

Is It Worth It?

Praying day after day, year after year, for our loved ones can become discouraging. We might wonder, *Is it worth it?*

For fifty-three years my grandparents, Russell and Florence Byrum *prayed daily by name*, for everyone who was born into, married into, or adopted into their extended family. When Grandpa died I felt as though someone had yanked not just the rug, but the whole floor, out from under me. Something I had stood on all my life was no longer there.

Shortly before Grandpa died, many people gathered around his bed. Grandma said later that as clearly as she could recall, by that time all except perhaps a dozen of those they had prayed for had accepted Christ. Grandma lived almost twenty years after his death, to the age of 94. As long as she was able, she continued to pray for folks. Grandma said that most of those did get saved during her lifetime.

How wonderful that God stores up our prayers. *"The four living creatures and the twenty-four elders fell down before the Lamb. Each one had a harp and they were holding golden bowls full of incense, which are the prayers of the saints."*[4]

I recently received an email from Jim, the son of Grandma's cousin. Many years ago, after finding Christ himself, he had added his prayers to those of my grandparents for his many brothers and sisters. Jim made sure he talked with each of them about their need for salvation. He said that all, except perhaps George, had turned their lives over to Christ before their death; one at the age of 91.

"Just two weeks ago," he wrote, "another of Florence and Russell's prayers was answered, probably nearly 80 plus years later. My brother, John. nearly ninety years old, was ill. We decided that we needed to visit as soon as we could.... I was able to ask him if he had ever accepted Christ as Savior. He had not, but said 'I guess I should someday.'

I asked, 'How about right now, John?' and explained how to pray a simple prayer, and then witnessed as John prayed—in his own words.

"I had written George (another brother) a letter urging him to make a decision and was on my way to visit him. I was hoping to be able to be reassured of his decision; but he died before I got there. I can only trust that our understanding of God's promises will include him."

A few weeks after this email arrived from Jim I finished going through the last box of my mom's

---

[4] Revelation 5:8

belongings. In that box, which I had avoided for two years since her death, I found an old letter from Jim's brother George to my mother which made it quite clear he had indeed accepted Christ in his latter years. What a joy it was for me to let Jim know that George is waiting for him in heaven along with the rest of their family.

It was reports like this that prompted Pete and me to make a commitment to pray regularly for extended family members. We include those we don't even know. We've created a list of the entire family tree to keep in our daily-reading Bible. That way we can make certain that at least several times a week everyone's name has been carried before God's throne in prayer. We've added to the list those not a part of the family but with whom God has given us special relationships. We've color-coded the list by categories: non-believers, those in spiritual leadership, those facing health problems, others with job and career needs, etc.

Some folks are surprised to learn that we are quite informal during our prayer-time. We sit in our easy chairs. We usually have worship music playing in the background.

One of us reads aloud a chapter or two from the Bible. Sometimes we stop to discuss a passage, or even look it up in another translation. Then we pray, while we're still sitting. God doesn't seem offended that we don't kneel. And my knees don't hurt when I sit. God doesn't seem to mind whether we have our eyes opened or closed. We pray both ways. Jesus apparently didn't care, for we read that *"taking the five loaves and the two fish and looking up to heaven, he gave thanks and broke the loaves."*[5] In at least three other passages of scripture we find Jesus talking to His Father with His eyes "looking up."[6]

---

[5] Mark 6:41
[6] Mark 11:41; 17:1, and Mark 7:34.

Even more unorthodox, perhaps, we sometimes pray while taking a walk or riding in the car. We also use normal terminology when we pray. No King James English for us. We address God in the same everyday English we use in normal conversations.

We often don't know what to pray, but we pray up and down the branches of the family tree several times a week. That takes us to the northwest, the east coast, the great lakes, Texas, Missouri, New Mexico, back to California, then to New Zealand, Lithuania, Europe, Malaysia, and beyond.

Often our prayers are petitions for individuals regarding specific things we know about: encouragement, provision, guidance. At other times we zero in on categories of needs, like praying for all the lost or sick, that God will strengthen and protect the marriages, or for wisdom and fortitude for those raising children. We try to be sensitive to how the Holy Spirit wants to lead our prayers. Occasionally we learn that the thing we prayed about that day or week is what God was working on in someone's life.

We share these details and methods only to inspire and challenge you to make the same commitment for your extended family. Perhaps you think there's already a family member praying for your relatives. Yet no doubt you have in-laws that person doesn't know who need your prayer.

You may not see them all make a decision for Christ in your lifetime. The story of the conversions in the Whitmore family, completed for that generation two decades after Grandma's death, is proof that God truly stores up our prayers and keeps on answering them.

During our early years of praying daily together we started praying for the future spouses of our children. One by one we've seen God bring His choice into their lives. Before our grandchildren were born we prayed not only for them but for those God chose to eventually become their husband or wife. One of the greatest blessings of this practice is that when a couple marries we already love that new in-law. With great grandchildren now growing up we enjoy praying for them and God's choice for their mate—even if they aren't born yet.

You may have your own private time of prayer each day. We encourage you to take the next step and make prayer together a daily appointment. You'll probably find like we have that having your spouse as a prayer partner is one of the greatest blessings your marriage can experience. How precious to realize that when Jesus said, "*Where two or three are gathered together in my name, there am I in the midst of them,*"[7] applies to marital prayer. No doubt you'll find yourself looking forward to it just as we do.

---

[7] Matthew 18:20

Chapter Thirteen

Getting Past the Past Through Forgiveness

I've dealt extensively with the area of forgiveness in *God's Gift of Friendship - Tools for Improving Relationships.*[8] Rather than repeat principles of forgiveness that apply to any relationship, we want to cover here those areas that affect the marriage relationship.

Start on the Right Foundation
Ideally a marriage begins with both a man and woman having a personal walk with God. They've saved themselves for one another—not just their bodies, but their hearts as well. During their time of engagement they are open and transparent about themselves: their dreams, their goals, and their pasts. Then they come together to form a covenant relationship and establish a family unit. They can expect that God can and will bless their marriage with peace, fulfillment, and contentment.

Few couples begin married life this way. Most have had little preparation for marriage. They've tasted of promiscuity. They have histories of various transgressions against God and their spouse-to-be. They hide their pasts from one another. Essentially they

---

[8] *God's Gift of Friendship – Tools for Improving Relations*, by Beverly Caruso, available from www.PeteandBevCaruso.com.

133

assume that when they walk down the aisle to say their vows everything will be like the fairy tales of childhood: "...and they lived happily ever after." This is like finding a plot of land, gathering building materials, and starting construction without taking time to lay a foundation. Jesus compared building such a structure to *"a foolish man who built his house on sand. The rains came down, the streams rose, and the winds blew and beat against that house, and it fell with a great crash."*[9]

Most of us need to go back and repair the structure of our marriage. But where would we begin?

We can spend time together before the Lord in prayer. Beginning with our life before we were married, we may need to repent of promiscuity of our youth, with others or with our eventual spouse. We need to ask God to help us to deal with those areas of our lives and our relationships of which we haven't repented.

Mark & Ellen had been high school sweethearts. They talked about marrying one another—some day. Then Ellen's parents announced that their family would be moving to another state. Ellen was not old enough to stay behind. She would have to move with them. What would the couple do? They couldn't get married without their parents' consent.

For several days they agonized. Finally they found a solution. Although they had not yet been intimate together, they decided that if Ellen got pregnant, her parents would have to let her marry Mark. Their plan worked. With a baby on the way, they were quickly married and Mark moved along with Ellen's family.

Things seemed to go fairly well in their marriage for the first few years. They had typical marital spats, some rough times. Although they were both young they thought they could make things work. After a

---

[9] Matthew 7:26-27

particularly difficult experience a neighbor introduced Mark and Ellen to Jesus.

For a while their marriage seemed to grow stronger. They had been Christians for several years when we found ourselves dealing with a particularly difficult problem in Mark and Ellen's marriage. In our counseling sessions with the couple, we seemed to hit a blockade. As we prayed together the Lord brought to Pete's mind something that we assumed had been settled long before. Had Mark and Ellen repented of the sin that resulted in the pregnancy?

Their response surprised both Pete and me. "Of course not! If we had not gotten pregnant, we wouldn't have been able to get married."

We sat stunned for several moments. Finally Pete said, "Don't you see that having sex before you were married was a sin?" Again they both denied that their actions had been wrong. In their thinking, the *good* result of the act made the act okay.

I wish I could say that in the end they repented and worked out their marital problems. The end of the story is still being lived out. It has been several years since the above counseling session. Mark and Ellen have been divorced for some time. As far as we can determine, neither of them ever repented of that fornication. It left a root of sin in their spirits—the product of unconfessed sin.

Another couple's story follows a more positive course. Matt and Ashley met as teenagers in their church. Although they both considered themselves good Christians, they both had close friendships with teens living compromising lives. When Matt and Ashley began spending time together it was without the permission of Ashley's parents. They became intimate and Ashley got pregnant.

Keeping It Fresh

They had both been working with the leadership as youth leaders-in-training and knew they had not met the standards. They were accountable to the church, so after telling their respective parents about the pregnancy they made an appointment with their pastor. They explained that rather than allow folks to learn through hearsay, they wanted to follow the right steps. They wanted to do what was right. They decided to go before the entire church. It was embarrassing, but they stood before the congregation and asked the forgiveness of everyone. The response was almost overwhelming as many surrounded them afterwards and offered hugs and words of forgiveness.

Matt and Ashley didn't want to marry only because a baby was coming. After several months of prayerful consideration, they decided to get married—after the baby was born. They had the usual adjustments to marriage, plus many that their early beginnings added to the mix. They tried to do things God's way as they understood it.

God led them to move to a new community. There they quickly moved into positions of spiritual leadership. Several years later they mentioned to a spiritual leader that they felt there might be something holding them back from the full blessing of God. They wanted to stand before God without any hindrance. If there was, they said, they'd like to know about it. A few weeks later the minister said God had impressed upon him that past rebellion was still lingering in their spirits. Matt and Ashley thought they had fully released rebellion, but if it was still there, they didn't want it to be passed on to their kids.

As they prayed together they realized they had never openly asked forgiveness of their family. They wrote the following in an email to each of their far away family members: parents, siblings, grandparents, and their aunts and uncles.

--

Dear Family,

As you know Ashley and I have been taking our relationship with our Father God to an extreme level. He has been moving greatly in our lives with favor, gifts and a refreshing in our family. In all He is doing we have found ourselves digging out the stones in our past and present as we plow the fields. We have been praying and believe that God has called us to a great ministry here. Over the past six months we have gone through many hard trials in our family. We began to pray for an exposure of open doors in our lives that might be hindering us. So God has revealed a particular issue from our past that we believe has not allowed us to walk in the full measure of His blessings.

With that said, we realized that we have not formally asked for your forgiveness for our rebellion before our marriage. And we are aware of the hardships that we put the whole family through. We ask that you would please forgive us for our actions while we were dating. We are sorry for the hurt and pain we caused you during that time. And in also allowing so much time to pass before we brought this forth. Please receive our hearts, humbled and open. We only wish that not another day goes by with this matter open.

If you have found it in your heart to forgive us, we do ask that you would respond with an email back. Please do not respond by pointing

out what we did wrong. But just to let us know
if this was well received.

Blessings to you, and love.

--

Matt and Ashley received replies from nearly
everyone. Typical was this one:

We forgave you in our hearts at the time you
confessed to the congregation. However, it is
good that you have specifically asked the
family members for forgiveness, not only for
your sakes, but for each of our sakes as well.

And so we both now convey to you our open
forgiveness for your attitudes, actions, and the
hurts we received as a result.

We love you both and are proud of the way
you have moved forward in your relationship
with one another and in your walks with God.
We expect that this difficult step now being
complete will close any door the enemy might
have been taking advantage of.

Go with God. Expect Him to bless you and
bless others and His Kingdom through you.

With all our love.

--

Ashley's mother expressed that this humble step
helped to close the door on the pain she had suffered
during that difficult year. Perhaps the most important
response was from one couple who had been especially
judgmental in their attitudes at the time of that first
baby's birth. The wife had told Matt and Ashley, "We
cannot bless this baby." In time the pain on both sides
had lessoned and the relationship had moved on with a
surface love.

Ashley says, "It was hurtful, but I had forgiven her.
Yet I felt they needed the release. Their response was
probably the best. They apologized and wrote, "I'm

really sorry for what I said. I'm blessed by seeing how your family has turned out." The relationship between the two couples is now healed.

It didn't take long for Matt and Ashley to see changes in both small and large areas of their lives, including their attitudes. Ashley says, "My thought processes, how I viewed situations, changed. I saw them differently now."

The couples' oldest child had been having frequent night terrors. He would cry and scream for no apparent reason. His parents couldn't settle him down. One night God awoke Matt and told him, "Go pray for your son. It's being released." He did so. There have been no terrors since. Ashley says, "He started showing a lot of affection. In fact, he has become very affectionate. We've seen a change in his temperament."

There is no way of knowing if the change in their son is connected to the steps of obedience Matt and Ashley took in clearing up things from the past. It is clear that their relationship continues to grow closer to one another and closer to God.

Other areas of unforgiveness can affect a marriage, not just premarital sex. Before moving forward in anyone's marriage relationship, it is wise to stop and deal with anything for which we have not repented, or anything for which we have not asked another's forgiveness.

A.W. Tozer wrote, "Sin is still the ancient enemy of the soul. It has never changed. We've got to deal firmly with sin in our lives. Let's remember that. The Apostle Paul wrote, *"The kingdom of God is not meat and drink, but righteousness, and peace, and joy in the Holy Ghost,"* (Romans 14:17). "Righteousness lies at the door of the kingdom of God. *'The soul that sinneth, it shall die.'* (Ezekiel 18:4, 20)."

Tozer went on to say, "This is not to preach sinless perfection. This is to say that every known sin is to be named, identified and repudiated, and that we must trust God for deliverance from it, so that there is no more sin anywhere in our lives. It is absolutely necessary that we deal thus, because God is a holy God and sin is on the throne of the world. So don't call your sins by some other name. If you're jealous, call it jealousy."[10]

We dealt with many couples during our thirty-five years as pastors, as well in the marriage seminars we teach. Additionally we've worked with missionaries and pastors. Without a doubt, unforgiveness is the root issue in the majority of marriage problems.

After we have dealt with sin, we can move forward with a clean heart expecting God to help us to keep our relationships clear and receive His blessings.

Let's look at other areas where unforgiveness might harm a marriage:

Vows and Promises

When we have a painful experience we sometimes tell ourselves something like, "I'll never let that happen to me again." Our self-promise might be even more specific: "I will never confide in that person again!" "I will never trust anyone from *that* country!" or, "*that* ethnic group!"

We've just made a vow. We may not view it that way, but God does. And if it was stated audibly, the forces of darkness have taken notice as well.

Should we then wonder why we have problems in certain areas of our marriage? If we ask God to shine the light of His love into every area of our lives, He will be

---

[10] *Five Vows for Spiritual Power*, by A.W. Tozer, Christian Publications, December 1990.

faithful. Sometimes we're surprised after such a prayer to remember a long forgotten vow.

We can ask God's forgiveness. If possible we can take action to fulfill the vow—if it was a valid one. Or to cancel it, if it was a foolish one. Then we can move on in victory in that area of our lives.

Married for the Wrong Reasons

When our children were young we began taking two young neighbor children, a brother and sister, to our church's mid-week *family night*. We felt these children would benefit from the activities for various age groups. Carolyn, another neighbor and a Christian, had befriended the children. She told us that these children were often left alone with no food to eat. The parents gave the children money to walk to the corner store to buy something to eat. That *something* was seldom nourishing food; often it consisted of chips, cookies, and soft drinks.

The children were unkempt and often visibly—and aromatically—unclean. The girl's classroom teacher told us she purchased socks for the children. When they arrived at school—always as early as the school doors opened—the teacher took the children to the restroom, washed their sockless feet and put socks on before replacing their shoes.

We wondered what kind of parents would be so negligent and leave such young children to fend for themselves. Eventually a situation arose where we had an excuse to ask the parents to come to our home for a visit.

After chatting a while the picture became clear. First the father told us he simply couldn't control the children. "I can't make them take a bath if they don't want to," he said. The mother, a dedicated career woman, admitted that she had never wanted to marry, much less have children. She did so because in her generation "that's what women did."

Few women today would likely repeat her actions. Still, many people do marry for the wrong reasons: to get out of her parents' home; to get out of another type of bad situation; because she is pregnant; because her biological clock is running down and she's desperate to have children; because he's lonely and someone finally showed an interest in him. We could easily add to the list.

When we counsel those who are in such marriages, they often say, "I married for the wrong reason. I didn't love him/her. God doesn't expect me to stay."

During our ministry in other countries we've talked with people who married because their parents arranged the marriage. Others didn't have a marriage ceremony because their culture expects that people will simply set up housekeeping and form a marriage.

We in the West forget that throughout history there have been many ways a man and woman have formed marriages besides making vows before a minister or judge. Some couples circle a fire together; others have their hands symbolically tied together during a ceremony.

No matter what method we came into our marriage, God looks upon the relationship as a marriage. He does not have a formula to which we must comply.

We can start right from where we are: married. We can repent of any sin that preceded it and ask God to do the work in us to make us the husband or wife He intended us to be.

Transference
Before I married Pete I didn't see anything at all in him like my dad. It didn't take long to find little

similarities between the two. After all, they were both men. These weren't the big hard-to-live-with faults, merely gestures, or word choices. Pete couldn't understand some of my responses to his innocent actions or words.

There had been elements of my dad's personality that made him hard to live with. That's probably true in many homes. Because some of those elements bothered not just me, but my mother and siblings, we sometimes openly talked about Dad—behind his back. I developed negative internal responses to many of Dad's ways.

One such characteristic was represented by a glass of milk. With four children in the family—according to our mother—someone, it seemed, spilled their milk, "at least once during every meal." That wasn't the worst of it. Whoever spilled the milk was immediately scolded by Dad. While Mom cleaned up the mess, Dad gave his usual emotionally charged lecture about being more careful. It didn't matter that we'd just heard it a few hours earlier. It didn't matter that the lecture changed nothing. I braced myself for that lecture at the first sign of a glass being knocked over.

We had only been married a few weeks. In the tiny kitchen of our apartment in the college Married Students' Dorm, I knocked over a glass of milk. I braced myself for a lecture from my new bridegroom. The next thing I knew Pete was laughing hysterically. Not used to being laughed at, I burst into tears. It was several long minutes before my loving husband could calm his distraught wife. Pete had seen my instantaneous reaction to the spilled glass of milk. The idea that I would be afraid of him had triggered the laughter.

Thankfully, I learned to laugh with Pete, and sometimes even at him.

What triggered my reaction to the spilled milk? It's called transference. I had responded with fear to Dad. Now I was reacting as though Pete would respond the way Dad always had. I was transferring my feelings to Pete.

There were other ways I reacted or responded to Pete that were inappropriate. Finally when I was in my thirties we recognized that I had been transferring feelings against my Dad onto Pete. I chose to forgive Dad for being the way he was and the many ways he had hurt me. I determined to talk with him during his next visit. What I found amazing was that as soon as I settled in my heart to forgive Dad, my responses to situations changed—even before I saw him again.

When Dad came for a visit several months later I asked to talk with him privately. I didn't elaborate when I forgave him. I simply said, "Dad, I haven't loved you the way a daughter should love her father. Will you forgive me?"

Some of us have people or circumstances in our lives that cannot be dealt with face-to-face. The person may have died, or the party involved can no longer be contacted. We can deal with these areas of unforgiveness in prayer. Or a representative—a substitute—for the offending party can hear our request for forgiveness.

Forgiving and Forgetting

In the book, *Restoring the Fallen*,[11] we see the ongoing process of asking for and extending forgiveness: "Demanding forgiveness is often a sign of nonrepentance. The repentant heart longs for forgiveness but rests in the knowledge that the only guaranteed

---

[11] *Restoring the Fallen*, by Earl & Sandy Wilson, Paul & Virginia Freiesen, and Larry & Nancy Paulson IVP Books, 1997, page 60.

forgiveness comes from the heavenly Father. The repentant heart prays for healing for those he or she has damaged and understands that healing takes time. He or she therefore exercises patience, longing for the day when the much-desired forgiveness will be extended. It is the responsibility of the restoree to admit doing wrong and to ask for forgiveness. Healing of relationships and forgiveness are part of God's mercy.

"The view of forgiveness that we are discussing runs against the grain. Prolonged pain indicates the degree of the hurt or injury, not the presence or absence of forgiveness. When pain comes to the surface, it reveals how severe the results of sin are; it does not mean that forgiveness has not occurred. Pain and forgiveness are different yet interrelated. Pain can continue after forgiveness. But the forgiveness, honestly given in due time, can help ease that pain.

"There is also a misguided notion that a person who has extended forgiveness will never speak of the offense again." Forgiveness, in fact, gives both the offender and the injured party the freedom to talk about the injury and its results.

Asking for Forgiveness

We not only need to forgive others. We must ask for forgiveness when we have been in the wrong. Pete learned this principle through much anguish. Here's his account:

After we'd been pastoring for 21 years the church gave us a sabbatical. We had a great year of ministry and learning. During that time God gave us an assignment, a tough assignment.

Bev and I were obedient and carried out that assignment. It wasn't easy. Especially when it didn't turn out as we expected it to. A lot of people were affected—and many were upset with us. Even our spiritual authorities.

Our reputation was wrecked. We had no ministry, no income. We moved in with our daughter's family and I got a secular job.

Often through the years, we would meet people who knew about our assignment from the Lord and they asked us what had happened. I would state the facts—I didn't embellish or bad mouth anyone. Just the facts.

After a while we started another church and pastored it for 14 years. But for twelve of those years we went through deep financial struggles. It was as though my pockets had holes in them. We cried out to God many times, asking what was wrong. I had been a man of faith. We had started the first church with no salary and God had always provided. Now we couldn't seem to get our chins above the water financially.

My brother John had told me he would never let me lose my house. Finally, when our house was in foreclosure, I went to him. In tears I asked him for help. He asked if we were tithing. Of course we were! John rescued us. But I still felt defeated.

Later that week I went to a three-day pastor's prayer summit. Each morning and evening we worshiped and prayed. No speaker, we just spent the time before the Lord.

In the afternoons we broke into groups of 12-15 men. Each man took a turn in a chair in the middle and was prayed for. Not me! I spent the time in the corner, weeping before the Lord, begging for an answer. I didn't even know which men were in that small group.

On the last afternoon they got me in the chair. I told them I needed a word from the Lord. After they prayed for me, I went to the dining room and sat next to a pastor I didn't know.

He had been in that afternoon session and asked if I got my word. I told him, "No."

He said, "I think I have it," and gave me an allegory that exposed hidden bitterness in my heart toward my spiritual leaders. I knew he was right. I determined in my heart that as soon as I got home I would make an appointment with my spiritual authority.

After a two-week wait for a meeting with him, I asked him to forgive me for the bitterness that was in my heart toward the leadership.

I had not known I had bitterness. Bev later told me that she had seen it all along and had tried to help me to see it. I would tell her, "I only state the facts. They ask me what happened and I tell them." I couldn't see that a spirit of bitterness was coming across and hurting God's flow in our lives.

What a joy to realize that as soon as I made the determination to ask for forgiveness, God recorded it in heaven and our finances were loosed. The change came immediately, even before I met with that spiritual leader.

Forgiving and Forging Ahead

Our friend Bishop Glenn Frazier illustrated this concept for his congregation by using a rope tying his hands together. He told them, "When a couple has a problem and one party doesn't forgive the other, it is as though that one is binding the hands of God. The unforgiveness binds the other person to the situation as well. They are going about their business, yet they are bound together. The only way to receive the full blessing of God is by cutting the ropes of unforgiveness. We can't cut the rope tying God's hands and preventing His blessing upon us until the rope between the two people is cut by forgiveness. The scripture explains it this way: *"Whenever you stand praying, if you have*

anything against anyone, forgive him and let it drop
(leave it, let it go), in order that your Father Who is in
heaven may also forgive you your [own] failings and
shortcomings and let them drop. But if you do not
forgive, neither will your Father in heaven forgive your
failings and shortcomings.[12]

How Does Forgiveness Work?

Forgiveness is a decision to trust God by faith. It has
nothing to do with how we feel. *"As your words are*
taught, they give light." [13] All we need to understand
about how to drive a car is to turn the key and guide the
wheel—we don't have to know how it happens. It's that
way with faith. We know His principle of forgiveness
works, we apply it and we're free.

Pete was talking with a woman past eighty years of
age who was filled with bitterness that affected all those
who knew her. She confessed to Pete that her father had
molested her when she was young. The pain of it had
poisoned her spirit all those years. Pete suggested that
she should forgive the man who violated her. After
making the decision to do so, she experienced a peace
she thought she would never know.

A pastor friend told us about a counseling experience
he had. The wife had deep bitterness toward her husband
and didn't want to forgive him. She believed she hadn't
done anything wrong and actually seemed to find
comfort in nursing her grudge.

The pastor asked her to read the Lord's Prayer aloud.
When she got to the part, *"Forgive us our debts, as we*
also have forgiven our debtors,"[14] tears began to flow.
At last she was able to see her sin of unforgiveness as

---

[12] Mark 11:22-26 Amplified bible
[13] Psalm 119:130
[14] Matthew 6:12

being just as wrong as those things she held against her husband. She had failed to notice that little word "as," which means "in the same way as."

Keep the Relationship Clean by Forgiving Immediately

We may think that by *stuffing it*, we're not giving place to bitterness. Rather we are merely pushing it down into our spirits. We are supposed to *"bear one another's burdens."*[15] That burden carried by the other person may be an immature attitude; a wounded spirit, or a broken heart, any of which can spill over into hurts toward us. An amazing aspect of this is that they usually don't even know they've hurt us. We are to do as Jesus did on the cross when He prayed, *"Father, forgive them for they do not know what they are doing."*[16] When we learn to *bear it* and not *stuff it*, the result will be a new ability to accept our spouse as he or she is, with their weaknesses and the hurts they inflict on us. We will be free to love them freely, just as Christ loves us.

Unreal Expectations

Author and marriage counselor, Gary D. Chapman, writes,[17] "Most couples I encounter in my counseling office have dreams of how wonderful their marriage would be if only …The *if only* statements almost always focus on things they wish their spouse would change:

- I wish she would get rid of some junk.
- I wish he'd help me keep the house cleaner.
- I wish she wouldn't worry so much.
- I wish he'd plan date nights once or twice a month.

---

[15] Galatians 6:2 New American Standard Bible
[16] Luke 23:34
[17] Christianity Today International/*Marriage Partnership* magazine. Fall 2007, Vol. 24, No. 3, Page 17

Keeping It Fresh

- I wish she'd stop being so critical.
- I wish he would express appreciation for what I do.
- I wish she would stop criticizing me in front of our children.
- I wish he would put things away when he finishes a project."

As these *if only* thoughts lie dormant in our spirits, we build unreal expectations in our minds. When our spouse cannot meet those expectations, we are disappointed and grow discontent.

If we'll be honest with ourselves, we'll realize that neither we nor our spouse can meet the other's expectations. We'll forgive them for our disappointment and readjust our way of thinking.

When we no longer hold false expectations, we can appreciate the little and big things our spouse says and does for us. We can focus on *being there* for one another and meeting each other's needs.

Chapter Fourteen

Meeting Your Wife's Needs

Most folks say the reason they married was because they fell in love. Closer to the truth is that most of us without realizing it get married in order to have our needs met—we believe we've found the best person to meet those needs. We're aware only of our own needs—for acceptance, companionship, security, sex. Maybe we should add: prestige, to be supported, etc. Yet our spouse has needs too—and he or she also married to get those needs met.

If our love is to last a lifetime, it must be other-centered, not self-centered. If we are only interested in getting our own needs met, that love will not last.

Earlier we looked at the difference between *Phileo Love (Friendship Love),* and *Agape Love (Sacrificial Love).* If we choose to love our spouse in a sacrificial way, we'll be concerned with meeting their needs.

The Needs of Women

Dr. James Dobson, the noted Christian psychologist surveyed 5000 women. In his book *What Wives Wish Their Husbands Knew About Women,*[1] he lists four

---

[1] *What Wives Wish Their Husbands Knew About Women,* Dr. James Dobson, Tyndale House Publishers, 1975.

151

common needs of women as their greatest source of depression:

- Low Self-Esteem
- Fatigue and Time Pressure
- Loneliness, Isolation and Boredom
- Lack of Romantic Love

In his book *His Needs, Her Needs,*[2] Willard Harley lists ten basic emotional needs. He writes, "I...made a revolutionary discovery that helped me understand why husbands and wives tended *not* to meet each other's most important emotional needs. Whenever I asked couples to list their needs according to what they needed most, men would list them one way and women the opposite way. Of the 10 emotional needs, the five listed as most important by men were usually the five least important for women, and vice-versa." Here is the list as ranked by most men and women:

Men	Women
Sexual Fulfillment	Affection
Recreational Companionship	Conversation
An Attractive Spouse	Honesty
Domestic Support	Financial Support
Admiration	Family Commitment

Harley goes on to say, "What an insight! It is no wonder that husbands and wives have so much difficulty meeting each other's needs: They lack empathy. They are willing to do for each other what they appreciate the most, but it turns out that their efforts are misdirected. What they appreciate the most, their spouses appreciate the least!"

---

[2] *His Needs, Her Needs:* Building an Affair-Proof Marriage, by Willard F. Harley, Jr., Fleming H. Revell Publishing, 2001.

By combining the lists from Dr. Dobson and Willard Harley, and his experience of fifty years as a husband and pastor, Pete lists eleven common needs of women:

- Affection
- Conversation
- Openness and Transparency
- Financial Security
- Self-Esteem
- Rest and Restoration
- Security
- An Understanding Attitude Toward Her
- Friendship
- Shared Responsibility for the Care and Training of the Children
- A Head to Administrate the Home

Pete is going to lead us as we look at the needs of the wife.

The Apostle Peter stipulates that a man must get to know his wife's needs. *"Husbands, dwell with them according to knowledge, giving honor to the wife, as unto the weaker vessel, and as being heirs together of the grace of life; that your prayers be not hindered."*[3] *[Emphasis mine]*

So the Bible tells us to study our wife—to live with her according to knowledge. Keep in mind that although all women share *basic common needs*, each woman has additional needs that differ from other women—that are *unique to her*.

This passage also speaks of a man honoring his wife. To honor is to attach high value to something or someone. Surely if we honor our wife, we'll want to meet her needs. Let's examine each of these needs common to women.

---

[3] 1 Peter 3:7 King James Version

1 – She Needs Affection

Let's admit it guys, almost all men are more affectionate before the wedding. However, for your wife, affection does not mean sex, nor even foreplay. You might be surprised to learn what affection means to your gal. Have you asked her?

Things women have described as affection include:
> Writing her a loving note
> Sending her flowers
> Holding her hand
> Calling for no reason
> Taking a walk with her
> Giving her a foot massage

For some women, the ultimate expression of love is to ask, "Would you like to go shopping together?" If so, we can choose to go with a happy, unhurried, patient attitude. Not on a hunting trip, but as a time to enjoy being together.

Almost all women mention touch as part of affection. Touch, it seems, has an enormous affect upon human behavior.

I loved the old TV show, Candid Camera. In one episode a coin was hidden in the coin return slot of a phone booth. Sorry for those of you too young to remember phone booths; I know they're archaic. There was a place at the bottom of the payphone where you could get your money back if your call didn't go through. For some reason, most users seemed to check the slot even if they did not have money due them. In this Candid Camera trick a coin was placed there as a gimmick. Sure enough, the caller would find the coin and walk away with a pleased grin. But the show's producer stationed a woman nearby who would approach the pleased person and ask if the caller had found her money.

The amazing—and amusing—factor: if the woman gently touched the person on the arm while asking for her money it would always be given to her. If not touched, the person always denied finding any money. The difference? Just a mere touch on the arm.

We guys are missing a huge benefit to our marriage if we overlook the touching element of our relationship with our wife. Researchers tell us that touching slows one's heart rate, lowers blood pressure, increases levels of serotonin—a brain chemical linked to the sense of well-being—and relaxes other bodily functions. It decreases levels of the stress hormone cortisol which can boost immunity.... An affirming touch from her husband sends an important message: "You are important to me; I'll protect you: I'm proud of you; I want to be close to you; I'm happy with you." All those things can be said with one gentle touch. What a wonderful gift God has given us in the gift of human touch. [4]

Hugging is a big part of affection for a woman, not just as a prelude to sex, but just because she enjoys it. One psychologist said, "We need four hugs a day for survival. We need eight hugs a day for maintenance, and twelve hugs a day for growth."[5]

Because women love to hug, a husband can cultivate an environment of affection by hugging his wife—often.

Kissing is also important to a woman. A study ordered by an insurance company in Germany on the value of a morning kiss found that:

---

[4] *God's Gift of Friendship – Tools for Improving Relationships*, by Beverly Caruso, available from www.PeteandBevCaruso.com.
[5] Virginia Satir, American Psychologist and Educator, 1916-1988

- The secret to a long and successful, healthy life was a morning kiss—that means it's important to you too, guys.
- Men who kissed their wives in the morning had fewer auto accidents on their way to work.
- Kissers missed less work than non-kissers. Maybe the bacterial exchange builds immunity.
- Men who kiss every morning earn 10-30% more money. Why? One doctor said, "It could be because he starts the day with a positive attitude."
- Men who kiss in the morning live five years longer than men who are stingy with their kisses.

In a very real sense, each time we take time to hug, snuggle, or cuddle—whether it's stopping when passing one another for a quick kiss, or we find our wife in the kitchen and wrap in one another's arms for a long hug, or we spoon in bed on a cold winter's night, or we reach across the car to hold her hand—we're making a deposit of love that reaps dividends in our relationship. Later, even much later, when we want to have complete intimacy those deposits are there to draw upon. We are more than merely friends, or partners, or roommates. We are constantly exchanging affection which only serves to help our love to keep on growing.

Everybody wins when we hug and kiss our wife. She feels loved, we rise in her image, and the children feel secure knowing Mom and Dad love one another.

2 - She Needs Conversation

How much conversation and affection did you two have when you were dating? Isn't it true that before you married her you talked to her, winning her over? She had no idea you were going to stop after the wedding.

Women need *daily* conversation. They have a deep need to converse—with you. Yet the average married

American couple spends *only 37 minutes* in meaningful conversation *a week.*

How much conversation does your wife need? You won't like the answer. Studies show that in successful marriages the couple talks together between *10 and 15 hours a week.*

When she says, "Honey, let's talk," you'd better stop and talk. Because *if you don't,* she will look to someone else for that need to be filled. It might not be another man—or maybe it will. It might be her sister or best friend. But her deepest need is to talk with you!

If she says, "Let's talk" the wrong answer is, "Sure! What you do want to talk about?" That's about the worst thing you could say. Her spirit will be wounded. Her response—even if she doesn't say it out loud—usually will be, "Well, if you don't know the answer to that question, I guess we don't have anything to talk about."

We men have this thing about solutions. If we think there's a problem, we look for a solution. Women don't communicate because they're looking for a solution. They communicate in order to share. They share their souls as they think out loud.

To help you understand how she feels, let's turn the tables. You say, "Honey, let's make love."

She says, "Why? Do you want to make a baby?" That's the equivalent answer to "What do you want to talk about?" It would mean her answer was focused on the ultimate purpose—having children. Yet that answer would aggravate you as a husband. You're just thinking, *I don't want to have a baby. I just want to be intimate with you.* Just as men find sex enjoyable just for the sake of doing it, so women find conversation enjoyable just for the sake of doing it.

So get it straight guys. When you ask, "What do you want to talk about?" She's going to be agitated. She'll be thinking, *"Look, I don't want a discussion; I don't want a solution to the world's problems. I just want to be intimate with you."*

If you have to be out of town, call her every single day—even if you can only afford to spend 2 minutes on the phone.

Also, keep in mind the admonition from the Apostle James: *"Everyone should be quick to listen."*[6]

Remember, following her need for affection, conversation is your wife's second greatest need in life. You can—and should—meet that need for her.

#3 - She Needs Openness and Transparency

When a husband is honest and open with his wife he provides her with a sense of security in their relationship. If she feels you keep secrets from her, she will be insecure. Some men feel they need privacy. But those men will get a lot of questions such as:" Where have you been?" "What were you doing?" or, "What's the matter?" This causes the husband to feel that she is always prying and nagging—with all her questions. She becomes even more insecure. The painful truth for her is better than the insecurity of half truths or hidden truths.

Your wife has a great need to know you—that's what transparency is.

- It's being known for who and what you really are
- It's knowing what you're doing
- It's telling how you feel about things
- It's sharing what your goals are
- It's admitting what your fears are

If you are struggling in some area of your life, tell her so. If things aren't going well in your work, tell her about it. You don't have to go into detail. But if you

---

[6] James 1:19

don't tell her these things, she will sense it. Yet without knowing what is wrong, she'll imagine things—probably the wrong things.

Love grows between two individuals when they are transparent with one another.

The Bible teaches that we should be *"speaking the truth in love"* to one another.[7]

You can provide your wife with a sense of closeness by:

- Taking time with her and giving her your full attention
- Being aware of her and her needs, even when in public
- Expressing affection without sexual intentions
- Planning surprises and doing the unexpected
- Keeping her informed of your finances, job changes, ideas for the future
- Praying regularly with her
- Sharing with her your feelings as well as factual information

#4 - She Needs Financial Security

The need for financial security is deep and strong for a woman. Remember that she has more connections between the left and right hemispheres in her brain than you do. We men may function day-to-day. She functions in the now and in the future. It all runs together for her. That's why she carries a purse and you only a wallet. She's prepared for any potential thing that might come her way. You only prepare for the moment.

Money problems are among the top reasons for divorce. Your wife needs to look out on the horizon and feel secure, that it's going to be OK.

---

[7] Ephesians 4:15

You young guys…
- Live within your means. Let your own income cover your living expenses. Then if your wife gets pregnant your household will be used to functioning on only one salary.
- Take out good life insurance so she knows she'll be taken care of if something should happen to you.
- Don't get into debt. Most young couples today would spend 33 years paying off their current debts, even if they didn't add any more to their current indebtedness.
- Have a savings account—even a small one will grow over time. Someone I'm close to began to put away $15 a week 45 years ago. He soon began to invest that. This year he's retiring very comfortably situated in his finances. I wish I'd known to do that back then.

Don't keep your wife in the dark about your financial status. This will help in several ways:
- She won't worry about the unknown.
- She will be able to adjust her spending accordingly.
- She will be able to encourage you—as she wants to do.

You may delegate to your wife the actual bookkeeping, the paying of bills, etc. But the *emotional weight* of the finances is to be carried by the husband, not the wife.

All of these steps: being debt free, having life insurance and a savings account, will provide your wife with a sense of financial security.

#5 - She Needs a Healthy Self-Esteem

Did you know that a husband determines his wife's self-esteem? He can cause her to feel like *a nothing* or he can produce a radiant, self-confident woman. It all depends upon how he treats her.

How can you produce a radiant wife? Through praise! The Amplified Bible says, *"Let every one of us make it a practice to edify, to strengthen, and to build up his neighbor."*[8] If we are commanded to do this to our neighbor, how much more should we apply this to our covenant wife. She needs positive declarations affirming her. Affirmation is something everyone needs. *"Let us eagerly pursue the up-building of one another."*[9] The world looks upon physical beauty as important. God tells us to emulate, or strive to be like, the beauty of God's temple.

Imagine what it would do to your wife's self-esteem if you would develop the habit of daily telling your wife that you see in her a godly character quality. Then you name that quality and give her an example of how you see it demonstrated in her life. By pointing out positive qualities when you see them in your wife, you can actually motivate her to become the person you and God want her to be.

To help you identify qualities in your wife (and children), you could make a copy of the following list[10] and carry it in your wallet. You can look at the list each day and be prepared to tell her about one each evening.

---

[8] Romans 15:2 Amplified Bible
[9] Romans 14:19
[10] From *Developing Godly Character in Children*, Hands to Help Publishing, available from www.PeteandBevCaruso.com

Major Character Qualities and their Sub-Qualities:

Brotherly Love
Acceptance of
    Others
Affection
Affirming
Compassion
Deference
Encouragement
Forgiveness
Friendliness
Gentleness
Hospitality
Patience
Tolerance

Faith
Adaptability
Belief
Confidence
Courage
Flexibility
Hopefulness
Optimism
Perseverance
Purposefulness
Security
Self-Confidence
Trusting

Fear of the Lord
Availability
Boldness
Deliberation
Determination
Firmness

Gratefulness
Humility
Respect for
    Authority
Reverence
Standing Against
    Peer Pressure
Yielding of
    Rights

Integrity
Alertness
Consistency
Dependability
Discipline
Endurance
Leadership
Maturity
Persuasiveness
Self-Acceptance
Trustworthiness

Joy
Appreciativeness
Cheerfulness
Contentment
Creativity
Enthusiasm
Humor
Thankfulness

Loyalty
Commitment
Fairness
Faithfulness

Obedience
Attentiveness
Cooperativeness
Meekness
Submissiveness

Responsibility
Cautiousness
Decisiveness
Diligence
Initiative
Nearness
Orderliness
Punctuality
Resourcefulness
Thoroughness
Thriftiness

Virtue
Consideration
Generosity
Goodness
Helpfulness
Kindness
Peacemaking
Purity
Self-Control
Sensitivity
Sincerity
Truthfulness

Wisdom
Discernment
Discretion
Justice

Some things to keep in mind about building your wife's self-esteem:

If you only compliment her looks, what will she have left in years to come when she knows she has lost the beauty of her youth?

- Tell your wife that you need her, that she meets your needs, that you value her opinions.
- Tell others in front of her how wonderful she is.
- Don't tell her she is fat, or slow, or a nag. Do something to help her overcome these areas. Support her in those areas of need.

One way to build self-esteem in your wife is to make sure that special occasions are planned and carried out with loving care.

Make Her Feel Special through Thoughtful Handling of Special Occasions

We have several key opportunities each year to make our wife feel special. These are: her birthday; the anniversary of our wedding; Valentine's Day; Mother's Day; and Christmas.

If we mishandle these occasions, it matters little how we try to build her up at other times.

If we wait until after work on her birthday and blurt out, "Uh oh, how do you want to celebrate?" Or if we make plans for something else on our wedding anniversary, we'll be in the doghouse for sure. It's almost impossible to redeem ourselves after such a blunder.

Plan ahead! - Some of the steps toward becoming a thoughtful and loving husband regarding special occasions include:

Enter all special days in your Day-Timer®. If necessary, make a notation several days in advance so you can make reservations, buy a gift, arrange a baby sitter, or whatever other preparations will be needed.

Keep in your wallet and update periodically, her:
- Sizes
- Favorite color
- Favorite perfume
- Favorite flowers
- Favorite recorded music / musicians
- Likes and dislikes
- Favorite flavors / snacks / indulgences
- Styles of clothes, furniture, decorating

Some stores carry small cards for your wallet for you to fill in.

Keep with you a running list of items and ideas. Don't rely on your memory. If she mentions something she wants or she shows enthusiasm over something, make a note of it—discretely without her knowing you're doing it—but before you forget it. Go back soon and buy it before it's sold out. Then hide it. You'll be glad you did when that special occasion rolls around.

Surprise her in some way. The whole thing doesn't have to be a surprise, but something should be.

Notice how she honors others: you, the children, her mom, her best friend. She would probably like to be treated in a similar way.

Ask a daughter or her best friend for ideas, for methods of honoring her.

Include the children in making plans when appropriate. They may have good suggestions, and it's good training for later in their lives.

Ask what she would like, but don't be bound by it. Use her suggestions for ideas to help you be creative.

Consider a gift of *doing* occasionally. Something she knows you would otherwise never get around to.

164

Remember: Most women love it when her man can be sentimental and honor her without being awkward about it. If you feel awkward, fake it until it becomes natural for you.

#6 - She Needs Rest and Restoration
According to Dr. Dobson's study, the second greatest source of depression is Fatigue and Time Pressure. Do you remember the passage in Ephesians Chapter Five where it says that *husbands are to cherish their wives?*

Most of us guys don't realize what it's like to be a woman with family responsibilities that press upon her from morning until night, day after day, without end. Even when she is asleep, a woman is aware that it is she who must respond to the needs of a sick or frightened child. We men come home from work and we can lay our responsibilities aside. if we choose we can veg out in front of the television or get lost in a Louis L'Amour book, or a game on the computer. Our wife can't.

Here are some questions we can ask ourself:
- Do I know my wife's limitations?
- Do I know her capabilities?
- Do I know where she is vulnerable?
- Do I know what demands and pressures she lives under?
- Do I know if she is eating right? enough? exercising? getting enough sleep?
- Do I know her fears and hang-ups such as: Fear of the unknown? Fear of what could happen to me?
- Does she have time once a week to do just what she wants to do?
- Do I know where she is with the Lord?

Keeping It Fresh

- How do I react at *that time* of the month? (A man can teach the whole family by how he deals with this issue.)
- In general, am I compassionate or critical?

#7 – She Needs Security
Security In Her Relationship with You - She needs to know that in your heart and mind, the marriage will not end until "death do us part."

Malachi records God's declaration that He hates divorce. Jesus reaffirmed that God views a marriage as a lifetime union. We need to eliminate from our thinking and our speech any possibility of divorce.

When both husband and wife know that divorce is not an option they can be assured that they can work out their differences and not risk losing one another. There may be quarrels and misunderstandings. She needs to know that with God's help, you WILL stay together and work it out.

Choosing to Limit Yourself to Your Own Wife
We men by nature are conquerors who would like to conquer any woman that attracts our interest. The greatest show of love we can give our wife is to choose to forsake all others, consciously limiting ourself to her: our eyes, our body, our thoughts, our whole heart. By going against our natural instincts we communicate clearly—I Love You!

A wife needs to know she is Number One in her husband's life.
- Not other women—or another woman
- Not his job
- Not football, golf, racquetball, or hunting
- Not his hobby

166

During the years we were pastoring, I usually spent Saturday evenings in my office putting together my final notes for the next day's sermon. One particularly stressful evening when our daughter was about to be married, our sons were fussing at each other. Bev phoned me in tears. It was clear she couldn't be consoled over the phone. I put down my pen and drove home immediately. Bev and I took a drive together and I listened. There were no problems to be fixed. I just listened. I let her know I cared that she was hurting. I must have held her in my arms there in the car for thirty or forty minutes after she finished crying and talking. She has since said that was a turning point in her *awareness* and *certainty* of my love for her. She now knew that she was more important than any sermon, or even my job as a pastor.

Security in Your Love for Her
Are you meeting all of the love-needs of your wife? Did you know that your wife actually has a need for five kinds of love?
- Companionship love
- Compassionate love
- Romantic love
- Affection love
- Passionate love
Let's take them one at a time

Companionship love - We've already covered. Be her friend, spend time with her. Do fun things together.

Compassionate love – This was illustrated in the story I just told you about that Saturday night. Your wife needs you to show care and concern about what she feels, and what she is going through. Not with a superior attitude, nor a demeaning one, but with compassion.

Affectionate Love - We already covered this under her first basic need – Affection

Romantic love - Let's face it. Women are romantics, and they have no intention of looking for a cure. God made them that way, so why should we fight it? Let's learn to meet this need.

Some men think of romance as only connected to the area of sex. Most women would like romance expanded far beyond that realm of their marriage. In fact, lack of romance as a whole has a dampening effect upon any effort at romance in the bedroom. Let's look at some issues that have an impact upon a woman's sense of romance:

We can defeat our own effort to be romantic with bad breath; thoughtlessness; poor manners. Do you live up to this description? *"Love is kind"[1] and "wisdom that comes from Heaven is first of all pure and full of quiet gentleness, then it is peace, loving and courteous. It allows discussion and is willing to yield to others; it is full of mercy and good deeds. It is whole hearted and straightforward and sincere."[2]*

Imagine this: Your wife works all day, comes home and prepares dinner, cleans up the kitchen, bathes the children, and gets them to bed. You've been reading the sports section of the paper or watching an action packed TV show, fully identifying with the main character. For the first time since she got home, she sits down to relax. You look over at her with a silly grin and say, "How about tonight, Honey?" She brushes straggly hair out of

---

[1] 1 Corinthians 13:4
[2] James 3:17 Living Bible

her eye, looks up wearily and sarcastically asks, "How about what tonight?"

An effective way to introduce and keep romance in your marriage is to have regular, frequent dates. A good goal to aim for is once a week.

Before looking at what a date is, let's look at what a date is not:

- It's not time spent with a group or another couple.
- It's not when you ask *her* to get the baby sitter and choose the restaurant.
- It's not spending the time discussing the children, finances, or other problems.
- It doesn't have to end with sex.
- It's not you watching other women rather than looking at your wife and interacting with her. Do you give her cause to wonder if she's still attractive to you? When you make remarks about how another woman is built, or she finds your eyes lingering, she may joke about it, but down inside you are planting seeds of doubt about her place in your heart.

So what is a date?

- It is spending time together and focusing on one another.
- It includes an element of the unexpected.
- It includes the impractical.
- It includes creativity.

How can we have a successful date?

Plan ahead. Treat her like a queen, she'll make you her king! You don't need to spend a fortune on your time together. A walk in the park or along a beach can form the basis for a wonderful memory.

Women are drawn to men because of their strength and manliness. But they are won over by their gentleness. Women love a real gentle – man. Do you know the history of that word?

- A man of rank or nobility
- A man of social position
- A man of good instincts, courteous and honorable

So mind your manners, guys! A woman needs a strong leader who is also compassionate. If a man is all strength and toughness, if his mannerisms are full of sarcastic teasing, and if he is rude, his wife will be downcast, unresponsive in lovemaking, and generally miserable.

Manners are not sissy or unmasculine or unnecessary. Manners are scriptural. Let's look at that verse again. *"Wisdom that comes from Heaven is first of all pure and full of quiet gentleness, then it is peace, loving and courteous. It allows discussion and is willing to yield to others; it is full of mercy and good deeds. It is whole hearted and straightforward and sincere."* [3] Here's yet another description of a godly man interacting with his wife: *"Have kind affection one to another, in honor preferring one another.*[4] True humility is recognizing our position, but taking a lower place. We're told to *"put on mercy, kindness, humility, meekness, patience."*[5]

So man is intended to be the strong leader in the marriage, but he is to do it as a gentleman. A man's leadership should bring security to his wife. A man should by his words and actions show that he is looking out for his wife's best interests.

Manners are not rigid rules that are used only at formal occasions. They are acts of kindness for everyday life. Not just for public settings, but also for private. Not just for show, but for those we love the most.

---

[3] James 3:27
[4] *Ephesians 12:10*
[5] Colossians 3:12

Poor Manners That Turn Off Romance

At the dinner table:

- Licking your knife, picking your teeth, chewing with an open mouth, or talking with food in your mouth.
- Sloppy or slouchy eating, belching, speed eating, grabbing, or barking orders. (We can practice saying and teach our children to say, "Please pass the _____)," instead of "gimme the _____."

At restaurants:

- Griping at the waitress, unreasonable demands, complaining about prices, not leaving an appropriate tip. (Christians have a bad reputation about poor tipping – just ask any waitress who works on Sundays).
- Failing to step up to the hostess and say, "Party of two please, name is _____." Then pull out the chair and seat your wife (and daughters, and any other women who don't have their men present.)

Manners for all times:

- Compliment those who serve you and when things look nice.
- Build good memories for your wife and children. They learn by watching.
- Say kind things; do kind things.
- Don't get impatient when your wife is struggling with the baby or children, or groceries. Help her.
- Don't go out to the car and lean on the horn; get in the house and help her get the family ready.
- Open doors for her. (My wife doesn't wait for me to open the car door. By the time we knew we wanted this in our lives, it was too late to change *her*.)
- Carry heavy items for her.

171

Keeping It Fresh

- Be aware of her in crowds and let her know you haven't forgotten her.
- Introduce her to your friends. Don't just leave her standing there to ask later, "Who was that guy?"
- Don't allow other men to meet her needs; you meet them first.

Now that we've looked at the importance of manners, let's get back to examining romantic love.

- It is creating an atmosphere of caring and loving. Think of it as—a stage that you set for the two of you to enjoy your relationship.
- It's something she needs on an on-going basis.
- It's not the same as passionate love but it should be present prior to and during sex in order for her to be fully satisfied sexually.
- It should *not* be limited to just before sex.
- It is showing your wife that you delight in her, that you cherish her.
- It is telling her she is the only one who can meet your needs.

Passionate Love - The final kind of love your wife needs from you. This is what the Bible calls: Knowing your wife. It is also called: sex; lovemaking; and by a host of other names. Yes, this is one of the kinds of love your wife needs. We'll be covering this a little later in a separate chapter.

#8 – She Needs an Understanding Attitude Toward Her

It's true that you'll never understand your wife. But you can have an understanding attitude toward her. The reason men can say they'll never understand women is that women don't understand themselves. A woman's body goes through a series of hormonal changes every month. This affects her moods, her view of herself, and of those around her.

We used to joke at our house that Bev was temporarily insane once a month. She even repeated the joke sometimes. It was only a joke, but we did try to avoid heavy responsibilities for her, and even put off making important decisions at that time. I'm glad that phase of her life is past.

A woman's perspective on any given subject will vary during that time. Just be careful about letting her know that you're being extra careful during that time. For many women, it only increases their edginess when faced with evidence that others are taking special notice.

Also, be understanding of your wife's sensitivities to certain topics. Get to know what those sensitive subjects are. Then have an understanding attitude even if you don't understand it. What might she be sensitive about?

- Her educational level
- Her parents or family
- Her weight – A study was done of two hundred women to find out what effect the emotions had on dieting. Half of the husbands were contacted without their wives knowledge and were asked to give their wives extra hugs during the dieting period. There were no other differences in the two groups of women. At the end of the time period, those who'd been getting extra hugs had lost significantly more weight. Not only that, they tended to keep it off better than those not receiving extra hugs.

Your wife has needs that perhaps no one else you know has. Find out what they are and be understanding of them.

#9 – She Needs Friendship

Dr. Dobson lists *loneliness, isolation and boredom* as the third source of depression in women. Your wife needs friendship. Who is your wife's best friend?

You can be her best friend. How? Communicate with her. She needs a friend to share her dreams, desires, and fantasies with. If you don't become that friend to her, she'll find someone else. That may be unhealthy for your marriage. It could be another man. It could be another woman, which could lead to an unwholesome relationship. We've seen this happen. I'm certainly not suggesting that every woman whose best friend is another woman is in an unhealthy relationship with her. Yet it is becoming increasingly common, even among Christians.

Why not become your wife's best friend? Or at least closer than you are now? You can start by showing a greater interest in her than in your job, sports, or TV.

But keep in mind that she does need friendships, not just with you, but with other women. Our society has short-circuited God's original provision for this need. In smaller communities, especially in earlier times, women saw each other daily. They went to the well and chatted, they marketed daily for their provisions, They took their surplus produce to the town bazaar and saw one another there. Women of old learned from one another, shared their lives with others in a natural, spontaneous setting.

Women today may see other women only in the work environment and at church. They usually have no relationship with those they see at the market and elsewhere. They have to take classes or make a date with their friends to have that feminine interaction.

Guys, see to it that your wife has time and opportunity to be with other women. Encourage her to develop friendships, especially older women. The Apostle Paul gave good advice to the young minister,

Titus: *"Teach the older women...to teach the younger women..."*[6i]

#10 – She Needs You to Share Responsibility for the Care and Training of the Children

God never intended for women to carry alone the weight of raising the family. God said of Abraham, *"I know him, that he will command his children and his household after him, and they shall keep the way of the Lord, to do justice and judgment; that the Lord may bring upon Abraham that which he hath spoken of him."*[7]

Your wife needs your participation in

- Preparing for childbirth
- Planning the care, instruction and spiritual care of the children
- Carrying out instruction and discipline of the children
- Having fun with the children

Have you ever considered this? When your wife must be away from home for a time, do you refer to your care of the children as babysitting? If so, why? Is she babysitting when she's home with them? It should be natural for you to be involved in the lives of your children.

#11 - A Head to Administrate the Home

We discussed the role of husband as the home's administrator in Chapter Four when I shared on the verses of Ephesians 5:23-33. Let's refresh our minds in light of this being a need in your wife's life. *"The husband is the head of the wife, even as Christ is the*

---

[6] Titus 2:3
[7] Genesis 18:19

head of the church: and he is the savior of the body. Husbands, love your wives, even as Christ also loved the church, and gave himself for it; that he might sanctify and cleanse it with the washing of water by the word, that he might present it to himself a glorious church. So ought men to love their wives as their own bodies. He that loves his wife loves himself. For this cause shall a man leave his father and mother, and shall be joined to his wife, and they two shall be one flesh. Let every one of you in particular so love his wife even as himself."

If you meet these needs of your wife, you'll have a happy wife and a fulfilling and satisfying marriage.

Look again at these eleven needs of your wife:

- Affection
- Conversation
- Openness and Transparency
- Financial Security
- Self-Esteem
- Rest and Restoration
- Security
- Friendship
- An Understanding Attitude Toward Her
- Shared Responsibility for the Care and Training of the Children
- A Head to Administrate the Home

Keep in mind that we're instructed to respect one another. *"Husbands in the same way be considerate with your wife as you live with her and treat her with respect."[8]*

---

[8] 1 Peter 3:7 New American Standard Bible

Chapter Fifteen

God and Finances

The way a husband and wife handle the issue of money can make or break their marriage. A New York State University study found that two thirds of studies about marriage problems listed the area of *Finances* as either the primary or secondary cause of marital conflict.[1] Some researchers say that problems with money ranks ahead of infidelity as the leading cause of divorce.

This is no surprise to God. After all, He included this topic in His Word. There are 2,350 verses in the Bible about money and possessions, nearly five times as many as are found on the subjects of either prayer or faith. Jesus Himself said more about money than any other subject.

If we are to enjoy happy and fulfilled marriages, we will guard our hearts and our minds, as well as our wallets, regarding our use of money.

Many good resources are available to help a couple learn to approach their finances according to God's

---

[1] From the article *Financial Harmony: A Key Component of Successful Marriage Relationship*, The Forum for Family and Consumer Issues, New York State University.

plan.[2] We can find some common themes in many of the resources available:

Steps Toward Financial Integrity

- Remember that men and women have different ways of thinking about finances. We are attracted to our spouse because we believe he or she can meet our needs. Feeling financially stable is high on a woman's list of needs. It is not her husband's ability to provide, nor the amount of money in the bank that is most important. She needs to know that her husband is concerned and involved, and that he puts his trust in God to meet their financial needs. She needs to know that she is not carrying alone the emotional weight of the family's financial situation.
- A couple who prays together about their finances will keep no secrets from one another. They will assess their debts, income, needs, and desires, then take them before the Lord and expect Him to guide and direct them to make wise decisions.
- A couple who gives God His portion can believe and expect God to keep His Word. *"A tithe of everything from the land, whether grain from the soil or fruit from the trees, belongs to the Lord; it is holy to the Lord."*[3] *"Bring the whole tithe into the storehouse, that there may be food in my house. 'Test me in this,' says the Lord Almighty, 'and see if I will not throw open the floodgates of heaven and pour out so much blessing that you will not have room enough for it.'"*[4] Some claim the tithe was only for the Old Testament period. However, Jesus

---

[2] Among the best are the teachings of Crown Financial Ministries, www.crown.org, 1 (800) 722-1976

[3] Leviticus 27:30

[4] Malachi 3:10

stood in the temple and watched the people as they gave their tithe commenting on their giving.

- Practice generosity. In both the Old and New Testaments we see that God is pleased with those who give beyond the tithe, an offering, freely from the heart. *"Give, and it will be given to you. A good measure, pressed down, shaken together and running over, will be poured into your lap. For with the measure you use, it will be measured to you."*[5] *"If your enemy is hungry, feed him; if he is thirsty, give him something to drink."*[6] *"He who has been stealing must steal no longer, but must work, doing something useful with his own hands, that he may have something to share with those in need."*[7]

- God takes our handling of money into account when evaluating our spiritual condition. *"Whoever can be trusted with very little can also be trusted with much, and whoever is dishonest with very little will also be dishonest with much. So if you have not been trustworthy in handling worldly wealth, who will trust you with true riches? And if you have not been trustworthy with someone else's property, who will give you property of your own?" "No servant can serve two masters. Either he will hate the one and love the other, or he will be devoted to the one and despise the other. You cannot serve both God and Money."*[8]

- Learn to live within your means and to be content. *"I have learned to be content whatever the circumstances. I know what it is to be in need, and I know what it is to have plenty. I have learned the*

---

[5] Luke 6:38
[6] Romans 12:20
[7] Ephesians 4:28
[8] Luke 16:10-13

secret of being content in any and every situation, whether well fed or hungry, whether living in plenty or in want. I can do everything through him who gives me strength."[9] God knows whom to bless with wealth; those who will be faithful despite a modest income, and those who will learn to trust Him with only little.

- Don't make comparisons with others. It's so easy to return from a lovely home furnished with expensive items and feel sorry for one's self. It's possible, though, to enjoy those lovely things to the fullest while there and return to a simpler home with total contentment. I know. I've lived it. I have friends who suffer miserably under those circumstances. The difference is a matter of believing that God knows what is best for each one and refraining from playing the comparison game. God's promise is that *"he will give you all you need from day to day if you live for him and make the Kingdom of God your primary concern."*[10]

- Get out of debt and stay out. This is perhaps the most difficult issue for families today. Whatever it takes, however much we must tighten our belts, the goal must be to erase debt and live within our means. In order to do this we may need to humble ourselves and seek counsel. Take care that those counselors follow God's Word: *"First seek the counsel of the Lord."*[11] *"The godly offer good counsel; they know what is right from wrong. They fill their hearts with God's law."*[12]

---

[9] Philippians 4:11-13
[10] Matthew 6:33
[11] 2 Chronicles 18:4
[12] Psalm 37:30-31 New Living Translation

- Examine every area of your life to make sure no area is out of God's order. When we are aligned with His Word we leave no room for Satan to wreak havoc.[13]
- Learn the various ways God meets folks' needs and ask Him to let you participate with Him in that provision. Loren Cunningham, founder of the international missionary organization, Youth With A Mission, calls this *God's Plan for Provision.*[14] Loren says that God planned some practical results from our generosity, including provision for special categories of people. Each of us falls into one of these categories.

The Breadwinners

God told Adam he would earn his bread by the sweat of his brow. The breadwinner category includes the majority of people—those who labor to produce goods or services. Most pastors and evangelists are in this class, because they provide a service for which they receive payment. This principle—of full-time ministers being worthy of salaries—was endorsed by Jesus[15] and by Paul.[16]

The Poor and Needy

The needs of the poor are to be provided through our generosity. Rather than taxing the population and redistributing wealth through impersonal government means, the Bible upholds our right to personal

---

[13] Ephesians 4:26-28

[14] From *Daring to Live on the Edge*, Chapter 7, by Loren Cunningham with Janice Rogers, YWAM Publishing, 1991 (Loren adds: "I am indebted to my friend, Rod Gerhart, for the delineation of these four categories, which I have adapted."

[15] Luke 10:7

[16] 1 Corinthians 9:7-14; 1 Timothy 5:17-18

ownership but reminds us to give generously to the poor and needy.

Jesus said that we will always have poor among us. There are various reasons for this—some poor people are innocent victims; others are poor because of wrong choices. But in any case, we are not to harden our hearts,[17] make excuses, or send them away empty-handed.[18] Jesus did not tell us to give only to the deserving poor. He did not say, "Give to him who asks of you...unless, of course, he is a welfare cheat or has been unwise in handling his finances." No, He said, "*Give to Him.*"[19] Giving is an act of mercy, and mercy is never deserved.

The Sent Ones

Another category of people Loren calls the "sent ones." He uses this term instead of "missionaries" because too often we narrowly interpret missionaries as people wearing pith helmets, preaching under the trees to natives in far-off jungle-lands. The original root for the word "missionary" meant "sent one."

The Manna People

Some people, for special purposes and callings of God, are directly supported by God. Like the Israelites receiving manna in the wilderness or Elijah being fed by ravens, this kind of direct provision from God is for a short time, in unusual circumstances, or for a dramatic demonstration of His power.

It is into this category God seems to have put *us* as a couple for long periods of our lives. We've heard from many friends and family members who have observed

---

[17] Deuteronomy 15:7,11; 1 John 3:17
[18] James 2:26
[19] Matthew 19:21; Mark 10:21

our lives, learned of God's amazing ways of providing for us, and told us in one way or another, "We knew that if God took care of you, He would take care of us."

When we gain God's perspective of finances and learn to trust Him to take care of us, and follow His guidance, we can rest in the assurance that He will do just that.

God is Our Provider, Not Our Jobs, Nor Our Abilities

The Scriptures teach us to look to God as our supplier. He alone can care for us. He has promised to do so.

In order to increase your faith, we would like to share some of the many ways God has taken care of us as a couple and a family throughout our fifty years of marriage.

Pete was still in Bible College and also serving as a youth pastor. His salary was meager, but so were our expenses. It was time for me to cook dinner, but with nothing to prepare. Pete seemed unperturbed. "Let's pray and ask the Lord to provide," he said calmly.

Pete had only begun to pray, reminding the Lord— and ourselves—that it was up to Him to meet our needs. I was having a hard time concentrating on the prayer. I looked up at nine-month-old Debbie playing on the floor of our tiny rented four room house. *We can do without food for a while, but what will we do about her needs?* I wondered. I was wishing I hadn't weaned her yet, at least she'd have milk.

Leaning back against the tattered sofa, my head touched the lace curtains and I glanced out the window. A black Cadillac was pulling up at the curb. I watched with fascination as a man from church walked around to the passenger side and pulled out a huge tray loaded with loaves of bread. As he approached our door, Pete's astounded face joined mine at the window.

We greeted our visitor with a mixture of excitement and consternation. He had to tip the huge tray to fit it through our doorway. "These were left over from the servicemen's center," he said. "I felt the Lord wanted me to bring them to you. There are also eggs and milk still in the car."

We expressed our gratitude and through embarrassed laughter shared with him about our unfinished prayer. After he left we made breakfast for supper and called it a feast of celebration.

I remembered the bread delivery about two years later as I set the table. We were now a family of four and pioneering a new church in a rural area of Southern California. Pete was now a senior in Bible College and we lived on his GI benefits and whatever else we prayed in. We had agreed when we started the church not to tell others of our needs.

Tonight we don't need plates, I silently told myself. *Salad plates and small bowls will be enough.* I emptied the can of green beans into a small pot and placed sliced canned peaches in the bowls. I hoped the meager meal would satisfy our hunger.

Pete chuckled as we held hands in a circle around the table and he led us in thanking the Lord for the food, the last food in the house. Debbie looked at her Daddy with pinched brows. She must have been wondering where the rest of the meal was. Little Mike was too young to realize this was a strange meal.

We told the story of the bread delivery wondering if Debbie could grasp its meaning. "This is all we have to eat tonight," I explained. "But God will provide food for tomorrow by the time we need it." I silently prayed, "Don't let us down, Lord."

Shortly after the children were tucked into bed we heard a rap at the door. There stood two friends with bulging brown sacks in each arm. I pondered as they helped us unload the groceries. *Should we tell them about our simple supper? Is it okay after the provision to tell about our need?*

Pete broke into laughter and spilled out the story. Our benefactors told us they were twice blessed. First while they shopped, sensing they were obeying God, then again upon learning of the timeliness of their arrival.

Breakfast the next morning was a celebration of thankfulness as we shared over bacon and eggs with Debbie and Mike how God had sent His provision once again.

Many additional times during those three years of pastoring with no salary God proved His faithfulness to supply for His children. But one incident remains etched deeper in my memory than any other. Perhaps it's because I still find it hard to believe.

I always had to pray in the money for my personal needs. I usually started praying a few weeks before I actually needed it. Not this time. Laundries with coin operated dry cleaning machines were a new concept. I placed Pete's suit and my wool skirts in the machine, added appropriate coins and sat nearby. I wanted to hang up the clothes before they could wrinkle so kept a close watch for the machine to stop. Other customers had left and I sat alone in the shop.

After the tumbling clothes came to a rest I opened the door and hung them, one-by-one, on hangers I'd brought from home. Then it happened. As I started to reach for a skirt I spotted something green. Reaching in, I picked up a twenty dollar bill.

Instinctively I glanced around the store for the person who had left it. No one in sight. Of course! I had been alone and watching the machine closely. Remembering that anything going through the cleaning process carries a chemical odor. I sniffed the bill; it had no odor. The bill was neatly folded in half, was flat, not crumpled as one would expect if it had been through the cleaning cycle.

All the way home I mentally rehearsed the events. I had been sitting where I could see the machine at all times. I was certain no one had been near the machine at any time.

After I told my incredible story to Pete he confirmed my conviction that the money could not have been in our clothes previously. Twenty dollars was too great an amount in the '60s to have been forgotten, and besides, neither of us had even held a twenty for weeks.

God added to our congregation and by the end of our third year the church had purchased property and we were receiving a small salary. Increases followed and eventually we didn't need to pray for our provisions "from God's hand to our mouths." With a comfortable salary we often forgot that God was behind the provision of a paycheck.

One Christmas season a couple of years later we learned what that throng gathered on the Sea of Galilee must have felt like in Jesus' day. Our youth group was returning from a day in the snow. They stopped at our house to sing carols for us—at suppertime. We knew they were hungry, but I had prepared only enough Sloppy Joes for the four of us. With only a quick shared glance Pete and I knew that we should serve them. We would find something else for ourselves after they left. We served the dozen or so young people plus their youth pastors. When some came back for seconds we were surprised neither the pot nor the package of buns was empty. After the group left we prepared to clean up only to find enough Sloppy Joes and buns left over for our family of four.

Mark was one of the men in Pete's leadership group. Each Thursday evening they gathered to discover God's ways of living the Christian life—they called it Discipleship Night. One particular evening Mark and Pete pulled into the church parking lot and parked side-by-side. Mark closed his car door with a definite attitude.

As they walked inside together Pete asked Mark what was bothering him. "It's my wife," he grumbled. "Every night she bugs me. 'We've got to get a bed for Lesley,' she nags. Pastor, the crib is borrowed and the owners have a new baby that needs the crib. But every night she reminds me, and every night I tell her we don't have the money for one."

Pete stopped and looked Mark in the eye. "It's so simple, Mark. She only wants to know you care. When you get home tonight, take her by the hand and ask her to forgive you for your lack of concern. Then pray and ask God together to provide a bed."

The following Thursday Mark enthusiastically told the rest of the guys about that conversation, then added, "After we prayed together it was only a matter of days before God provided a new bed for our little girl!"

After pioneering two churches, pastoring a total of thirty-five years, and ministering in over forty countries, we are again experiencing living "from God's hand to our mouths." It's an exciting life to never know how a bill will be paid, nor when. We are daily reminded that it is God who provides: not man; not a salary; not our labors. He is the same Jehovah Jireh that provided a ram for Abraham, bread for a youth pastor, groceries for a young pastoral family, a crisp twenty dollar bill for a young pastor's wife, enough food to feed a youth group, and a bed for a toddler. He is the provider of all good things.

Perhaps you will never be in such a situation; though in all likelihood you could. When that time comes, remember your Provider. God wants you always to look to Him and not to your job, your credit cards, or your abilities. He has promised to take care of His own and to supply all our needs.[20]

You may be thinking, "Living by faith like you've just described is risky business." It may feel that way. We want to assure you that whether you receive a salary, own your own business, or have no job right now, putting your faith in a God Who promises to love and care for us is not risky. What is risky is counting only on ourselves, our jobs, or our government to supply our needs.

---

[20] Philippians 4:19

Chapter Sixteen

Lovemaking, God's Gift to Marriage

We've come to a subject some readers have waited for—or perhaps skipped to. Others have dreaded it and may want to skip this chapter altogether. We want to encourage you to be open to a new understanding of this subject—a subject God is not only interested in, He is the one Who thought it up.

Sex Doesn't Embarrass God

We should not be ashamed to discuss that which God was not ashamed to create. We tend to think God is shy about sex. But it was God who made certain that the book we call the Song of Solomon—or more appropriately—the *Song of Songs,* is in our Bible. In that lovely book we see illustrated God's perspective of sex.

God intended for sex—lovemaking—to be a source of joy, fulfillment, contentment, and comfort to both the man and the woman. *"Marriage should be honored by all, and the marriage bed kept pure, for God will judge the adulterer and all the sexually immoral."[1]*

Let's make a comparison: The New Testament gives us an interesting picture of the church, *"Brothers and sisters, when you come together, everyone has a hymn,*

---

[1] Hebrews 13:4

Keeping It Fresh

or a word of instruction, a revelation, a tongue or interpretation. All of these must be done for the strengthening of the church."[2] Do you see the balance there, of singing, worship, teaching or preaching, and spiritual gifts. Our marriages are to be balanced too.

If we make worship the essential part of a church service, it will kill the church. But if we neglect worship, we also will kill the church. It's that way also with the Gifts of the Spirit and the believer. If we make them essential, we kill the spirit of the believer. If we neglect the believer's gifts, we'll also kill the spirit of the believer. If we make *sex* essential in marriage, we will kill the marriage. If we neglect sex, we also will kill the marriage.

A wise man said, "Great and godly sexual activity starts between the ears before it ever happens between the sheets."[3]

Both Men and Women Have a Need for Sexual Fulfillment

When we put the other person's desires, pleasures, and needs before our own, we validate their worth. When we put our own needs before theirs, or when we withhold ourselves from them, we essentially say, "you have no worth."

Loneliness is a pre-fall emotion. Before Adam and Eve sinned, God was lonely; so He made man. Adam was lonely, so God made Eve. The *act of marriage* is intended to show us the intimacy and abandonment of Jesus and His Bride.

We must check our motive, asking ourself, "Do I want to bring fulfillment and delight to the one I love?

---

[2] 1 Corinthians 14:26.
[3] From the handout sheet for February 10, 2008, Pastor Curt Seaburg of Victory Church, Lancaster, PA, USA.

190

Or do I just want to meet my own needs?" How do we treat our spouses? Could the husband say, "When I have her, I don't really have her?" or can she say, "When I have him, I don't really have him?"

Do we neutralize our own efforts by failing to take the necessary time and effort to prepare our minds, our bodies, our environment, and our lover? The marriage bed should be the safest place on earth for both of us. Are we working to make it that for our spouse?

Too often we try to bring unity to the marriage by force of our will upon our spouse. If we want unity of spirit with our spouse (that is: genuine affection which underlies all else), we will not work merely toward unity of our function or our flesh. Rather, we will work toward becoming one by choosing to have a loving attitude toward them.

Many of us put out effort—great effort—with the busyness of other things in life, in order to fill the void we should find first in our relationship with God, then with our spouse. Whether it's our job, our hobby, our friends, even our ministry—we should not be pouring ourselves into activities as a substitute for those two most precious relationships—between ourself and God, and between ourself and our husband or wife.

So Many Misconceptions About Sex!

Experts say that young people today get their information about sex from a wide variety of sources. Many of those sources didn't exist a generation or two ago. Most of them are providing a distorted view of God's original plan: far too little from church, maybe a little more from father, then school, mother, media, peers, TV, the internet.

God gave a lovely picture of married love in the book of the *Song of Solomon*. God chose to use poetic language rather than medical terms or straight data:

"You have stolen my heart with one glance of your eyes. Turn your eyes away from me for they overwhelm me."[4] As King Solomon records the reflections of his youthful Queen, Shulamith, we see that God intends sex to be a gift to a married couple, a source of pleasure and fulfillment.

As she approaches their wedding feast and their first night together, Shulamith says that she looks forward with joy to married love. Although later in the Song we're given a glimpse of her thoughts as she describes herself as a virgin-bride, yet she is not inhibited, *"May he kiss me with the kisses of his mouth,"* then, *"your love is better than wine..."* and finally, *"we will rejoice and be glad."*[5] When they reach the bridal chamber she even describes to him what she would enjoy, *"Let his left hand be under my head, and his right hand embrace me."*[6]

There are some clear and important lessons we can learn from Solomon and Shulamith:

Lessons for Women from Shulamith

If we are not loving our husband in an active, participating way, he isn't a happy man. He may not admit it, but his perception of himself as a man is closely tied to the way he sees himself as a lover. Sex makes a man feel wanted. Sex is a primal form of giving of himself. Rejecting a man's sexual overtures is like rejecting him.

---

[4] Song of Solomon 4:9
[5] Song of Solomon 1:2 New American Standard Bible
[6] Song of Solomon 2:6 King James Version

If we must say "no," on a particular occasion, we can say *no* to sex, not our husband. We must let him know it's not him we're rejecting, but that *now* is simply not the right time.

We could compare the importance of sex for a man with the importance of communication for a woman. If a husband refused to talk to his wife for several weeks she'd be distressed. So it is with men and sex. Depriving him of intimacy at the physical level is emasculating him.

Attitude Makes a Huge Difference

The first lesson we can learn from Shulamith is to maintain a positive attitude. Let's personalize this and ask ourself some questions about our own attitude toward sex:

What do I think about lovemaking? Shulamith was aware that God had designed it. Her attitude was healthy.

What do I think about myself? Shulamith saw herself as a Rose of Sharon and a Lily of the Valley, both were common, but lovely, flowers in Palestine.

What do I think of my husband? Do I find fault? Criticize? Even if this is only in my thought life, it will affect our lovemaking. Shulamith said of Solomon, *"My beloved is white and ruddy, the chiefest of ten thousand. His head is as the most fine gold, his locks are bushy, and black as a raven. His eyes are as the eyes of doves by the rivers of waters, washed with milk, and fitly set. His cheeks are as a bed of spices, as sweet flowers, his lips like lilies, dropping sweet smelling myrrh. His hands are as gold rings set with byrl, his belly is as bright ivory overlaid with sapphires. His legs are as pillars of marble, set upon sockets of fine gold. His mouth is most sweet, yes, he is altogether lovely and this is my friend."*[7] To him, she said, *"How handsome you are my beloved, and so pleasant."* Notice that she compliments his lovemaking skills, *"like an apple tree among the trees of the forest, so is my beloved among the young men."*[8]

Do I think about my husband sexually or do I just think, *What a nice guy he is*? Do I think of how great it is to make love with him, or do I think of him as that wonderful father and provider? It is perfectly holy to think erotic thoughts about our husband. It's in the Bible.

What do I think my husband thinks about me? This is probably the most important. *"He has taken me to the banquet hall, and his banner over me is love."*[9] Shulamith doesn't view Solomon as using her, but rather as loving her. Look at what she says about him, *"I belong to my lover and his desire is for me."* [10] And, *"I will give you my love."*[11]

Relax, and Let Go of Inhibitions

"May my beloved come into his garden and eat its choice fruits,"[12] Shulamith said. In today's vernacular that might be, "Come and get me."

Men are Stimulated by Sight

Men respond to visual stimuli much more than women. Some time later in their marriage, Shulamith danced for Solomon in their private place together. Solomon's description of her indicates she had little or no clothing on.

---

[7] Song of Solomon 5:10-16
[8] Song of Solomon 2:3
[9] Song of Solomon 2:4
[10] Song of Solomon 7:10
[11] Song of Solomon 7:12 New American Standard Bible
[12] Song of Solomon 4:16 New American Standard Bible

It's not that a man wants his wife to have *the ideal body*. He wants to *enjoy* her body—the ordinary getting dressed and undressed in his presence. The glimpse of her in the shower. The way she looks in clothing she wears only for his eyes. His sense of manhood is reinforced by her indulgence of this need and her seductive interaction with him.

"What attracts men to women is their femininity, and femininity isn't only about appearance, it's also about behaviors. Looking womanly and behaving sweetly and flirtatiously are gifts wives give to their husbands. This gift communicates that the husband is seen as a man, not just a fixit guy, the breadwinner, or the sperm donor. And if it's romancing a wife is hungering for, presenting oneself as an appealing "woman" will get more romancing than presenting oneself s only as a child-care worker, or house cleaner, or the other wage earner."[13]

You are the Responder, So Respond

Chances are our moods and emotions will catch up with our actions. Throughout The Song's charming love story, we see Shulamith responding to Solomon's advances. We've all experienced this *responding phenomenon* in other settings. A common one is when we've had an extremely full week. Saturday's demands have left no time to prepare for Sunday. We wake up thinking, *I'd sure like to skip church today*. But we have responsibilities at church. We drag ourselves out of bed, get the family ready and pull ourselves together. About halfway through the service we realize that we feel better than we would have if we had stayed in bed. It's that way with making love when we aren't in the mood.

---

[13] *The Proper Care and Feeding of Husbands*, by Dr. Laura Schlessinger, Harper Collins Publishers, 2004.

If we'll just put ourselves into it, we'll find that we can enjoy it, and maybe even be fulfilled.

Communicate Freely with Your Love

At a bridal shower the guests were asked to share one word of advice with the bride. My favorite is, "Share your thoughts and feelings with God and your husband regularly." Shulamith told Solomon that she was homesick for the countryside. He responded by planning a trip to take her back to Lebanon for a visit.[14]

What about the things needing to be said that might bruise our spouse's ego? Debra Taylor, a certified sex therapist offers some practical advice for communicating about sex. "To talk honestly about our sexuality, sexual preferences, fears, feelings about our bodies, struggles, joys—this is intimacy, deep friendship with trust and faithfulness.

It's important for each couple to negotiate how they are going to *talk* about their sexual relationship together. Whenever we approach our spouse with information that could be perceived as criticism, we need to be respectful and thoughtful.

"It's best to have a sexual talk away from actual lovemaking. Arrange some uninterrupted "just us" time for conversation (the kids are in bed, or get a babysitter and go somewhere private), and then bring up your desire: "I've been thinking about our lovemaking ..." is one way to start. Be careful not to use the word *but* ("I usually like what we do, *but* ..."). The word *and* works better ("I enjoy our lovemaking *and* I've been thinking about some things I'd like to do with you ...").

"Positive suggestions are more useful than vague or negative comments. Affirmations and sincere compliments help alleviate fears of rejection or

---

[14] Song of Solomon 7:11

criticism. When you talk together about your sexuality, you're talking about one of the core parts of your person; you're on holy ground. Be mindful of where you are and speak respectfully—as you would want your husband [or wife] to be respectful and kind to you."[15]

Dr. Michael Sytsma adds some practical suggestions: "You may also want to try subtle direction and reward. This works best when the two of you are in a playful sexual mood. In those times, you could say, 'Oooh. Would you _____ (fill in your pointer)?' When he does, make a big deal about it. Moan and let him know, 'You haven't done that before. It feels really good tonight.' That kind of affirmation speaks powerfully to most men.

"During the relaxed time after sex, tell him how you wouldn't want that every time, but you enjoyed him trying that this time: 'Our typical routine is comfortable and feels good. Sometimes trying something different is also good. You're a great lover.'"[16]

Pray—Yes—Pray About Sex

It may seem awkward at first, but remember, God created sex. Repeatedly we *hear* Shulamith talking about her love for Solomon. Her audience is not identified. It seems she may have been talking to God. Surely we can talk to the One Who created sex and gave us this intimate gift of love.

Get Rid of Wrong Thinking

Don't be afraid your husband will demand sex all the time if you give yourself freely to him. Shulamith said,

---

[15] Debra Taylor, MFT, certified Christian sex therapist and co-author of *Secrets of Eve,* Thomas Nelson.
[16] Michael Sytsma, Ph.D., a minister and founder of Building Intimate Marriages, www.intimatemarriage.org

"I have become in his eyes like one bringing contentment."[17] She certainly didn't feel he was demanding too much of her. Rather, he brought her contentment. One reason men appear to be obsessed with sex is because they get so little of it from their wives. If a man has not eaten a meal in five days, every time he passes the refrigerator, food will be all he can think about. Like food, sex isn't the most important thing in life. If we are not totally available to him, sex can become an obsession for our husband. We can plan time for making love. It doesn't have to be scheduled, but we can learn our husband's patterns. When we're aware that he's going to want to make love we can make ourself ready, emotionally, physically and psychologically.

Become Skilled in Sexual Techniques

The late Mrs. Billy Graham told a group of women, "A prostitute is skilled in all the techniques of giving sexual pleasure to a man she does not even know or love. If prostitutes can do that for men they don't even know or love, just for money, surely we should be even more skilled in giving sexual pleasure to our husbands whom we do love." It is biblical for a wife to be a skillful lover to her husband. Shulamith said to Solomon, *"My lover, at our door is every delicacy that I have stored up for you. Come away, my lover."*[18]

Be Creative!

Solomon said of Shulamith, *"How beautiful is your love, my bride. How much better is your love than wine."*[19] When we learn to abandon ourself to our

---

[17] Song of Solomon 8:10
[18] Song of Solomon 7:13
[19] Song of Solomon 4:10

husband, we are expressing the love between Christ and His Bride.

God gives us an interesting picture of marital love in Genesis. After Sarah died Abraham sent his servant to bring Isaac a wife. It seems that as soon as Rebekah arrived, *"Isaac brought her into the tent of his mother Sarah, and he married Rebekah. So she became his wife, and he loved her;* **and Isaac was comforted** *after his mother's death."*[20] God wants us to know that marital love is a source of comfort to a man.

Lessons from Solomon for Men:

For Her It's Not Just Physical

Great sex for your wife is life with you as a whole, not just the physical act. How you treat her all day, each day, in every way, will affect your love life. Again and again in The Song, we see Solomon romancing his wife. He pours words of admiration and praise upon her.

Don't Trust Your Instincts

Learn that your instincts will not teach you your wife's needs. In the New Testament we read, *"You husbands likewise, live with your wives in an understanding way..."*[21] The verb translated "live with" is consistently translated in the ancient Septuagint translation of the Bible as "Have sexual intercourse with." The phrase "in an understanding way" implies acquiring knowledge and insight through a process of personal investigation. Thus an interpretive and expanded paraphrase of the verse might read: "You husbands likewise, have sexual intercourse with your

---

[20] Genesis 24:67
[21] I Peter 3:7

wife in a way that is based upon insight gathered from personal investigation of *her* needs." When a husband learns to make love to his wife, putting her feelings and needs first, he is living out the love and care of Jesus for His bride.

Women Need Romance

The Song of Solomon seems to teach that romantic love has at least six ingredients.

• **Romance includes an element of the unexpected**. Anything that is repeated over and over loses its romantic value. Together we were teaching an adult Sunday School class. The topic was marital love. One woman blurted out, "I know he'll kiss me, here, here and here in about five seconds and think I'm supposed to be ready for sex." The entire class laughed, but we all know this scenario is far too common. If our love making has become routine and predictable our wife probably doesn't feel romanced. Solomon surprised Shulamith by building their bedroom of cedars of Lebanon.[22] It must have looked much like home to her and pleased her a great deal.

• **Romance includes words** that tell her that she is loved; words that convey that you love to look at her, ...touch her, ...smell her, ...listen to her. Words that tell her you respect her and enjoy being with her. President and Mrs. Ronald Reagan were perhaps the most famous romantic couple in recent time. When they had to be apart, she would tuck love notes among his clothes to be found later. One of *his* love notes to *her* is on display at his Presidential Library in Simi Valley, California. It reads: "I love you mucher and mucher than that you are

---

[22] Song of Solomon 1:17

my cuddly wuddly little pink Honey Pot. XXXX Guess Who?"

• **Romance includes time**. Sex can be rushed, lovemaking cannot. Remember that making love doesn't mean just intercourse. Practice self-control. Solomon created an atmosphere; he romanced his wife with tenderness. He delighted her and gave her time to desire him. He waited until *she* signaled him that she was ready.[23] She said *"May my beloved come into his garden and eat its choice fruits."*[24] Remember guys, it usually takes longer for a woman to be ready for intercourse than it does her husband.

• **Romance includes the impractical**—Arriving with sixty soldiers dressed for battle was not a practical way to escort his bride the 200 miles from the mountains of Lebanon to Jerusalem, but it must have been romantic to Shulamith. A woman may need a new vacuum cleaner or bathrobe, but Valentine's Day is not the best time to give her one, unless the robe is feminine, sheer and...impractical.

• **Romance is personal**—Solomon's description of Shulimith is extremely personal. Most women would be impressed if their husband broke into a love song. But if the song has another woman's name in it, he's likely to be given a cold shoulder—unless he replaces that name with *her* name! Or better still, his pet name for her.

• **Romance is blind**—Young women of Solomon's day were sheltered from the sun's rays. Fair skin was considered more lovely than tanned. Yet Solomon looked beyond Shulimith's tanned complexion and saw only beauty. *"All beautiful you are, my darling; there is*

---

[23] Song of Solomon 4:15
[24] Song of Solomon 4:16 King James Version

no flaw in you. "[25] Spouses see one another at their worst; love blindly sees only their beauty.

What Arouses a Woman is Not Primarily Visual

More important to her than anything visual is your gentleness and having you focus on her, that is, *tuning everything else out*, and allowing her to be responsive. An area that is difficult for many men, but is far more important to a woman than most men can imagine are the words spoken by her husband. Most women are aroused by words, coupled with the right tone of voice. Silent, wordless sex may be good for men, but the right words *at the right time* during lovemaking can enhance your wife's pleasure more than another gentle touch.

She Needs to Believe You Love All of Her

Here is one of the most difficult concepts for wives to get across to their husbands. Women often feel merely used by their husband just for his sexual release. In order for her to respond with passion she needs to feel that he takes pleasure in her body for its *own* sake, looking at it, touching it, enjoying it. In addition she needs to be assured that he loves and respects her mind, emotions and spirit that are in her body. If she feels he's doing something from mere routine, she will lose her passion and will likely find it difficult to regain it.

Protect Her Privacy

Solomon treated Shulamith with dignity, therefore she felt safe to abandon herself to his love. If a wife fears others can see them, or hear them, or that her husband might discuss their love-life with others, a wife is inhibited from freedom in their sex-life.

---

[25] Song of Solomon 4:6

Mind Your Manners

Be aware of bad manners and offensive odors. While daydreaming about Solomon's qualities, Shulamith said, *"He is outstanding among ten thousand."*[26] And, *"His mouth is full of sweetness and he is wholly desirable."*[27] He had no body odor or bad breath.

Take Care During Her Cool Down Time

Affection after intercourse can be vital to a woman's satisfaction. A woman can actually feel lonely after making love if her husband turns over and falls asleep immediately or gets up to watch TV. Most women want to be held for a while. In fact, the stroking and sweet words, the holding and tenderness she receives after intercourse can have more meaning to her. He's not doing it merely to prime her emotions for sex.

Communicate Freely, Even About Sex

Did you notice the many words exchanged between Solomon and Shulamith?

Communication in general—not just when you want sex—is vital to your wife. She needs to know you desire to share yourself and understand her.

Verbal expression from you during foreplay is important to her. Notice how Solomon excites his wife, using poetic language, by telling her how desirable she is to him. *"How beautiful you are my darling. How beautiful you are! Your eyes are like doves behind your veil. Your hair is like a flock of goats that have descended from Mount Gilead. Your teeth are like a flock of newly shorn ewes which have come from their washing. Your lips are like a scarlet thread and your*

---

[26] Song of Solomon 5:10
[27] Song of Solomon 5:16

mouth is lovely. Your neck is like a tower of David...your two breasts are like two fawns, twins of a gazelle which feed among the lilies."[28]

Reuter's released a news article[29] by Patricia Reaney telling about researchers at the University of Groningen in the Netherlands who used scans to analyze brain activity during intercourse in both men and women. The article reported, "When women genuinely achieved an orgasm, areas of the brain involved in fear and emotion were deactivated. Those areas stayed alert however when women were faking it. The deactivation of these important parts of the brain might be the most important thing necessary to have an orgasm. It means that if you are fearful or at a very high level of anxiety, then it is very difficult to have sex because you really have to let yourself   go."

This article cites scientific proof that women need to be relaxed and free of anxiety and fear in order to enjoy sex. The research indicates male orgasm is not as directly related to emotions as female orgasm is. This explains why a husband is not as directly affected by words as his wife is, and why most men don't understand the importance of speaking words of affection and erotica to her. But like a chain reaction the wife's excitement usually excites her husband so they both end up sharing an elevated level of passion for each other when he takes the time to share sweet words with her.

- If you have difficulty using words during lovemaking:
- Memorize passages from the Song of Solomon in a modern translation.

---

[28] Song of Solomon 4:1-5
[29] Reuters, June 20, 2005

- Memorize poetry. You can find expressions of love in greetings cards, novels, etc.
- Make a list of the things you like about her. Go over your list during the day so you'll be prepared to tell her about one or two.

Negative comments at any time can have a lasting affect on your wife's response and enjoyment. Never put down your wife's body. Instead, if something needs to be said, choose a time totally separate from a sexual setting and make your remarks in a positive way.

Verbal expression afterward helps her feel complete—not used.

Let's Review

Companionship love - Solomon listened to her, walked with her.

Compassionate love - He cared that Shulamith was homesick.

Romantic love – Solomon was a true romantic.

Affectionate love - Do you only reach out to touch and hold her when you want sexual release?

Passionate love - It's much easier for a wife to be responsive to passionate love when her other four love needs have been met.

Be Her Protector and Leader

Shulamith was asked, *"Where has your beloved gone? Where has your beloved turned?"*[30] She answered, *"My beloved has gone down to his garden.. .to pasture his flock in the gardens."*[31] It seems significant that Shulamith views her husband, the King, as a shepherd who pastures his flock. Despite Solomon's

---

[30] Song of Solomon 6:1
[31] Song of Solomon 6:2

shortcomings—and what husband doesn't have any?—Solomon made his wife to feel totally loved, protected and cared for. She saw him not only as Israel's shepherd, but as her shepherd. There are two major characteristics of a shepherd. He is a protector and a leader. Elements of protection embrace sacrificial expressions of love. The fact that the shepherd dedicated his life to his flock, even to the point of possibly losing his life, demonstrated emphatically his care and concern for them. A good husband must also be willing to *"lay down his life daily"* for his wife. If a wife feels approved, loved and cared for, sex will be a comfort to her as well as to her husband.

Poetic Language to Caution Men

"Drink water from your own cistern, running water from your own well. Should your springs overflow in the streets, your streams of water in the public squares? Let them be yours alone, never to be shared with strangers. May your fountain be blessed, and may you rejoice in the wife of your youth. A loving doe, a graceful deer—may her breasts satisfy you always, may you ever be captivated by her love. Why be captivated, my son, by an adulteress? Why embrace the bosom of another man's wife? For a man's ways are in full view of the LORD, and he examines all his paths."[32] This passage compares the man's experience with a 'strange woman' (the Hebrew word shaga)—translated ravaged—with his experience with his wife (rava)—translated satisfied. The former means "to go astray, to stray, to err," the latter means "to be satiated or saturated, to have or drink one's fill." The word "let" in that verse means "allow it to be." A loving husband can choose to be satisfied with

---

[32] Proverbs 5:15-21

everything about his wife: her complexion, her size, and her weight.

Beyond *The Song* for Both Husband and Wife

We don't see these in the *Song of Solomon* but want to share from our years of marriage and pastoring.

Guard against fantasy - Fantasy is making things up in one's mind that cannot be reality. Indulging in fantasy will result in being dissatisfied with reality. Why? No one can live up to another person's fantasy.

Don't be afraid to show affection in front of your children or even friends. They are bombarded with unhealthy, sinful displays; they need to see godly affection at appropriate times in appropriate ways, between married couples.

Children need to learn at a young age that they are not a part of the marriage, they're a part of the family.

Pornography is merely having one adulterous affair after another - with absent strangers. There are many counterfeits for what God intends us to find in the marriage bed: alcohol, drugs, work, pornography, and in some cultures—kava or other substitutes. God's intention is that we find our sexual fulfillment in our relationship with our husband or wife. *"Marriage should be honored by all, and the marriage bed kept pure, for God will judge the adulterer and all the sexually immoral."*[33]

---

[33] Hebrews 13:4.

207

Depriving a spouse of their sexual needs is another form of infidelity. "When we normally think of infidelity, we think of a spouse having an emotional and/or sexual relationship outside of the marriage, whether with a "real honey" or a "synthetic honey" on the Internet. That is an obvious breach of marital vows as well as a violation of the Ten Commandments. However, don't the marital vows include and imply words like love, honor, protect, care for, and so forth? So when one breaches those vows by neglect, is that not also a form of infidelity? Perhaps we should start looking at the act of intentionally depriving a spouse of his legitimate needs as infidelity, too, because it stems from being unfaithful to the intent of the vows."[34]

God placed upon the man the responsibility for the health of the marriage and home—this includes their sex life. He made the man first to stand alone. He made woman out of the man's side to be a helpmate. Therefore, it is a man's responsibility to love and care for his wife even as he takes care of his own self. Let's look again at that passage in Ephesians Chapter Five: *"Husbands, love your wives, just as Christ loved the church and gave himself up for her to make her holy, cleansing her by the washing with water through the word, and to present her to himself as a radiant church, without stain or wrinkle or any other blemish, but holy and blameless. In this same way, husbands ought to love their wives as their own bodies. He who loves his wife loves himself. After all, no one ever hated his own body, but he feeds and cares for it, just as Christ does the church – for we are member of his body. However, each one of you also must love his wife as he loves himself, and the wife must respect her husband."*

---

[34] *The Proper Care and Feeding of Husbands*, by Dr. Laura Schlessinger, Harper Collins Publishers, 2004.

Now let's take a look at some of scientific findings related to love and sex.

Love is Difficult to Describe.

"How would a scientist describe love? It probably wouldn't be as romantic as a poet's or lyricist's description," wrote Helen Fisher. [35] She goes on, "I fancy it would be something like this: *"Love is a chemical attraction between two people, influenced by environmental and cultural factors, for the purposes of finding a suitable mate to further one's family line."* Simple as that.

Fisher, an anthropologist at Rutgers University and one of the most well-known researchers in the science of love, would go a bit further and define it in three sequential phases: Lust; Attraction; and Attachment. At each stage, there are identifiable patterns within a person's brain, hormonal balances, and neuro-transmitters. Thus, love can be scientifically identified by examining the chemicals in your brain."

Others have described the three stages as:

Lust – What drives us to find a partner; it's related to bursts of testosterone.

Romantic love – It is biochemically similar to obsessive-compulsive disorder: serotonin, dopamine, norepinephrine – blood cells are involved, platelet abnormality. The heart races, pupils dilate, there's light sweat. The person is elated, giddy, and can't sleep or eat. Dopamine, the pleasure chemical gives us a high. It can be stimulated artificially by alcohol and drugs. It

---

[35] *Why We Love: The Nature and Chemistry of Romantic Love*, by Helen Fisher, Henry Holt and Co., 2004

involved PEA—the hormone of libido, and increased sex drive. It's in Viagra and chocolate and gets oxytocin flowing.

Long-Term Love - The person has a calm, secure feeling of attachment for the long-term. It triggers oxytocin—the cuddling hormone.

Many of us define *intimacy* in marriage as sex and while that is certainly a valuable part of the marriage relationship, a healthy marriage has to have emotional intimacy to go the distance.

What exactly is emotional intimacy? Emotional intimacy occurs when there is enough *trust* and *communication* between a husband and wife that it allows both to share their innermost self. Deep emotional intimacy is when we feel *wholly accepted*, *respected*, and *admired* in the eyes of our mate even when they know our innermost struggles and failures. Emotional intimacy fosters compassion and support, providing a firm foundation for a marriage to last a lifetime.

Too many marriages today try to exist without emotional intimacy. Over time a marriage lacking intimacy will become empty, lifeless, and the husband and wife will find distance in their relationship. Emotional intimacy is the glue that holds relationships together, yet it is challenging for many of us to experience.[36]

We can strengthen our sexual relationship by nurturing our marriage relationship as a whole. And by strengthening our sexual relationship, the rest of our lives will be enriched.

----

[36] *Emotional Intimacy*, by Jill Savage, 2006 online at www.hearts-at-home.org.

Chapter Seventeen

Out to Destroy Our Marriages

Satan is out to destroy marriages—all marriages. Although most of us know this we fail to apply it to our own lives. Satan wants to destroy *your* marriage.

We saw in Chapter Four—God's Marriage Analogy—that God views marriage so highly He uses it as a picture of the relationship between Christ and the church. God intended marriage to be a haven for two individuals who would make a lifetime commitment to one another, who could bring new lives into the home to nurture and to train for service in God's kingdom.

All of this is contrary to the goals of our adversary—the one who sought to raise himself up above God and take His place.[1] If Satan can destroy our marriages, he can thwart God's plan. Satan is working against marriages universally, through the various spheres of influence: especially the arts & media, entertainment, education, and our government. He is also working to destroy individual marriages—yours and ours. In fact, everything good that God has for us, Satan wants to disrupt or pervert.

---

[1] Isaiah 14:12, 13

211

He's After Our Relationship with Jesus

When we are followers of Christ, every part of our lives are vulnerable to Satan's attack. He wants to cause a rift in our relationship with Christ. If he can't get us to sin openly, he'll try to get us to compromise. If that doesn't work he'll try to undermine our relationships. What relationship is most important to us—and to God? The one between husband and wife.

He Wants Non-Christians to Witness the Failure of Our Marriage

We Christians easily forget that the world is watching, and not just those Christians in the public eye. Unbelievers are watching us regular folks too. Some of them rejoice when they see the marriages of Christians fail. They think it vindicates their own failings,[2] and confirms that Jesus doesn't make a difference in lives after all.

Others are not necessarily unbelievers. As my elderly cousin once told me, "I'm not an unbeliever, I'm just a doubter." Al continued his doubting, and his seeking. And he kept watching us. After his ninetieth birthday he let me know that he was no longer a doubter. He had watched three generations of believers and finally became one himself.

Because our marriages are to be a reflection of Jesus and the Church, Satan sets out to mess up our marriage relationship. He wants those watching, including our children, to see misery and hatred.

---

[2] John 3:19

He Wants Us to Be Weak and Ineffective in God's Kingdom

Another reason Satan wants our marriage to fail is that it can keep us spiritually weak. If we're caught up in the struggles of a shaky marriage, we are less effective for God and His kingdom.

We're Fighting a Spiritual Battle

We need God's help to keep our marriages healthy. Our fight is not hopeless. Yes, there are evil attacks against Christian marriages and families, but *"our struggle is not against flesh and blood, but against the rulers, against the authorities, against the powers of this dark world and against the spiritual forces of evil in the heavenly realms."*[3] God has promised that *"the weapons we fight with are not the weapons of the world. On the contrary, they have divine power to demolish strongholds."*[4]

In *our* marriage, when we are having difficulty communicating, or when we can't have a meeting of minds, we suspect that Satan is at work. One of us will often stop, look at the other and say something like, "I think we're in a spiritual battle here."

It's easy then to join our hands, remind the Lord and ourselves of our love for Him and each other. Then we tell our adversary to "get outta here." OK, it's more likely worded, "Satan, in the name of Jesus, leave now. You have no part in us because we are God's children. We know you are a trespasser and we have authority over you. Be gone" It's truly amazing what happens when our spiritual enemy has been given his marching orders. Whatever the problem was, it is no longer a

---

[3] Ephesians 6:12
[4] 2 Corinthians 10:4

problem. Sometimes we even laugh at how ridiculous the tension between us was.

How does our enemy work against our marriage? As Bob and Yvonne Turnbull point out,

"Satan is a master of deception. If he can get you disappointed, or worse, discouraged about your mate—you know saying things like, "How come my mate never.....? or, "I know a lot of people who would appreciate me more than my mate does," thoughts like that—then the evil one has just stolen your joy.

"His next crafty step is to get you looking around for a better deal, and he makes you think that just possibly he has a better answer for your marriage than God does. Simply put, it's deception; yet look at the thousands who fall for it every year. Every day. At times the deception can be subtle, such as through encouraging you to put all your time and energy into your children or your work and spending less and less time with your mate. Or he entices you with someone else who seems to be so caring. Often when these deceptions occur in our lives, instead of drawing closer to God and seeking His help, we pull an Adam and Eve and run and hide from Him, as they did when they suddenly realized they were naked....

"We knew that God had a wonderful working plan for our marriage, just as He does for yours, if you're married. That plan is found in the latter part of our paraphrased John 10:10: "I (Jesus) have come that Christian marriages may have life, and have it to the full." That's what happens to a marriage that is truly yielded to the Lord. It is a completely full life. It takes three to have a championship marriage – the Lord as the coach and the husband and wife as the team players.

"We found that when we placed God at the center of our marriage it made a major difference.

"We know what we're doing wrong. It seems that when we're ashamed of not following God's plan, the bond between God and us is disrupted. Then hiding can become more frequent if these matters aren't dealt with through forgiveness." [5]

A Three-Fold Cord

A beautiful picture lesson is found in a seldom quoted book of the Old Testament, Ecclesiastes.[6]

"Two are better than one, because they have a good return for their work:

If one falls down, his friend can help him up. But pity the man who falls and has no one to help him up!

Also, if two lie down together, they will keep warm. But how can one keep warm alone?

Though one may be overpowered, two can defend themselves.

A cord of three strands is not quickly broken."

Within a marriage that is integrally interwoven with God, we can find: someone to help us when we're down; someone to be a true companion; someone to help us fight off our common enemy and protect our backside. The key is to truly include God in the relationship. Just as one takes hold of three strands and braids them together so that they become enfolded in one another: the husband, the wife, and God. When we become so much a part of one another and God becomes a part of us—our enemy cannot gain the victory.

You may be thinking, "That's all well and good if your husband or wife is a Christian. But mine would never join me in taking authority over the enemy; in

---

[5] Bob and Yvonne Turnbull, in their monthly email newsletter, *Evil Attacks Against Christian Marriages and Families.*

[6] Ecclesiastes 4:9-12

fact, I think he (or she) is on the enemy's side, though he would never admit it." This may be true. However even when one is married to an unbeliever, the believer can take authority over the enemy regarding their marriage.

Married to an Unbeliever—or a Doubter

Speaking of being married to an unbeliever, a passage in First Peter offers insight for any wife whose husband is not living according to God's plan. Although it refers to an *unbelieving husband*, it applies as well to a *believing husband* who is lacking in some areas of his Christian life. *"Wives...be submissive to your husbands so that, if any of them do not believe the word, they may be won over without words by the behavior of their wives, when they see the purity and reverence of your lives. Your beauty should not come from outward adornment, such as braided hair and the wearing of gold jewelry and fine clothes. Instead, it should be that of your inner self, the unfading beauty of a gentle and quiet spirit, which is of great worth in God's sight. For this is the way the holy women of the past who put their hope in God used to make themselves beautiful. They were submissive to their own husbands, like Sarah, who obeyed Abraham and called him her master. You are her daughters if you do what is right and do not give way to fear."[7]*

Such a wife would do well to refrain from preaching to her husband. By focusing on becoming a godly woman she will be working with God and thwarting the work of the enemy against the marriage. We believe the same principle would apply to the husband of an unbelieving wife.

The key to winning the battle for our marriage is to be ever mindful that Satan never gives up in his

---

[7] 1 Peter 3:1-6

attempts to defeat us. We must be diligent to practice the principles God established for husbands and wives; to put our spouse first after our relationship with God; and to keep Christ as the integral element in our marriage.

Keeping It Fresh

Chapter Eighteen

Deciding Whom to Marry

Someone asked ten-year-old Alan how one knows whom to marry. "You got to find somebody who likes the same stuff. Like, if you like sports, she should like it that you like sports, and she should keep the chips and dip coming."[1] Smart kid!

A neighboring pastor expressed his thoughts so bluntly that I had to write it down: "A young woman leaves a man who has provided her with love, acceptance, shelter, food, security, and far more for nearly twenty years, to marry a young twit who has nothing to offer her except promises. Love is not only blind, it is downright stupid."[2]

Perhaps you don't believe that. You're sure you've found your Prince Charming who will make you the happiest woman in the world. Or you're in love with the most beautiful girl you've ever met and you're certain she will meet your every need.

Just maybe, you're more like we were. We were afraid of marrying the wrong person. Pete's parents

---

[1] *Finding the Love of Your Life*, Neil Warren, Focus On the Family Publishing, 1992, p. 48.
[2] Pastor Bruce Goddard, in a Sunday sermon at Faith Baptist Church, Lake Elsinore, CA.

divorced when he was only eleven. Bev's parents divorced after she was married following thirty difficult years together. Yes, both of us were so afraid of making the big mistake that we were reluctant to get married. Let us tell you our story. We'll start with Bev's account:

I was the third child born to a Christian couple. They both loved the Lord but they sure didn't know how to create a healthy marriage. Dad was blissfully happy in the marriage, Mom was joylessly miserable. By the time I was fourteen years old, I was determined I would not make the same mistake. I told Mom I was never going to get married. She wisely responded, "Honey, it doesn't have to be like this. I didn't know I should pray about who I should marry. Your Dad just swept me off my feet and I married him. I guess I was in love with love."

That night I began praying for the one God wanted me to marry, and I did so every night before going to sleep. Sometimes I prayed that if he was not already a Christian, that God would save him. I also prayed for each of the guys I dated, just in case he was the one. Three years later I realized that I was praying for the same man twice each day: for my boyfriend Pete, and the one I was to marry.

Pete and I were married six months after we met. Our first Thanksgiving together was a special one: my first holiday meal with his extended Italian-American family. I was amazed when spaghetti and meatballs were brought on heaping plates. *My family always has turkey and all the trimmings*, I thought. *This is going to be interesting*. It was a large helping, but I was determined to eat every bite.

To my astonishment, turkey and all the trimmings followed the pasta, then salad and bread, then nuts and fruit, and finally a dessert. Only the women of the house left the table—in almost four hours.

On the way home Pete and I laughed about my limited capacity for food. It was then that I remembered the previous Thanksgiving. I asked, "Did anything unusual happen to you a year ago?" He thought only a moment then launched into his recollections:

"The first scripture I memorized at the recommendation of my spiritual mentor was, *'Seek ye first the kingdom of God his righteousness, and all these things shall be added unto you.'*[3] "I was in the Army, stationed in Germany. I had arrived there as a new Christian. I'd had quite a worldly background, so I was eager to follow the Lord in every area of life, especially regarding dating and marriage. Early in my Christian walk I had promised the Lord I would let Him choose my wife for me. 'Just put her in my path, Lord,' I prayed. 'I can't make such an important decision for myself. I'm willing to be single; but you know I want to be married.' I renewed that commitment and request each day for three years.

"In Germany in that year of 1957, Thanksgiving turkey was plopped onto my metal Army tray by strangers who saw this day as no different from the next. It was a far cry from the large family gathering taking place at my sister's home back in California. Homesickness grabbed me by the throat and squeezed tight.

"Suddenly I remembered the cute *fraulein*—what was her name?—who worked just off base. I decided I'd sin, just today. I determined to take her for a date, to a movie, then to bed. I was certain she was available, and willing.

"After dinner I took her to her apartment building. I was still wondering what her name was, and was

---

[3] Matthew 6:33 King James Version

embarrassed to ask, considering my intentions. Just inside the first of a double set of doors was a row of mailboxes. Perhaps this was my chance to learn her name. As she put the key into the lock of the interior doors, I turned briefly and pointed to the boxes. "Which mailbox is yours?" I asked as I heard the latch open. I quickly turned back for the answer, but she was gone.

"Quickly I looked through the glass door, searching the hallway and the stairs with my eyes. Instinctively I opened the outer door and looked up and down the street, but I knew she couldn't have exited that fast, or silently. It was impossible, but she was nowhere to be seen. There was nothing left to do but to return to my barracks.""

As Pete finished his story on that, our first Thanksgiving together, he looked across the car into my eyes. Maybe he was wondering if I was offended by the account. I sat in wonderment for a full minute, until he finally inquired, "Why did you ask?"

Now it was time for my story. I told him that, as I had the previous three Thanksgiving weekends, I attended a youth convention in Los Angeles. During the first service a burden of prayer had come over me. I didn't know what I was to pray for. I only knew that the man I had been praying for daily for three years—the one I referred to in my prayers as *the man I'm going to marry*—was in need of prayer. I explained that because of watching my own parent's unhealthy marriage, I was fearful of marriage, and had decided that I would make sure I had God's choice, or remain single forever.

At that youth convention, for a day-and-a-half, I spent my time praying, every waking minute that I wasn't in the common meetings. Then suddenly during one of the services the prayer burden lifted. I didn't know why; I didn't know what had happened. I went back to being a carefree teenager at a youth convention.

We rode silently south along Interstate 5 for a while. Both of us knew the treasure we had uncovered. Even before we had met, God had used a high school senior to pray her future husband out of a situation where he was about to sin.

We have shared this story many times, in churches, in our Marriage Enrichment Seminars, and when we teach in Youth With A Mission's Discipleship Training Schools. We encourage young people to ask God for His choice of a husband or wife for them, and we encourage parents to pray for the future spouses of their own children.

Like Alan in our opening story, another 10-year-old, Kirsten, seemed to speak of my story: "No person really decides before they grow up who they're going to marry. God decides it all way before, and you get to find out later who you're stuck with." I've long teased Pete that he had no choice but to love me. God put us together. He did a good job of it. Our love just keeps on growing, for more than fifty years.

Marry for the Right Reason

Why do I want to get married? might be a better question to start with. By examining some potential answers we can better focus on the *whom* question:

- "I'm expected to" – This is perhaps the worst reason. Remember our neighbor with the two neglected children?
- "There's a baby on the way" – No longer does society force a couple to marry because of a pregnancy. Yet many couples turn one mistake into two by forming a marriage that never should have been.

Keeping It Fresh

- "To get out of a bad situation" – Whether to get out of the parents' house or to put a roof over one's head, a worse situation is likely to result.
- "I'm divorced and want to start a new life" – Unless a person has learned from his or her mistakes from the first marriage, those mistakes will likely be repeated in the next.
- "My spouse died and I'm lonely" – Loneliness can cloud one's perspective and cause emotional blindness.

Reluctant Brides

Researchers admit that most people get cold feet at least some time before the wedding day arrives. This is quite normal. Sadly, many who start toward the altar realize they are truly making a mistake. Some are wise enough to break the engagement. It's painful, it's embarrassing. But the alternative is worse. I know a bride who told one of her bridesmaids while they were dressing for the wedding, "I know I'm making a mistake." After asking a few questions, the bridesmaid said, "Don't go through with it. You aren't married yet. It's not too late."

"People are already arriving, the bride protested. "We've already opened many gifts. I can't call it off now."

You guessed it. Within two years the couple were divorced. This was a Christian couple. Presumably they had prayed about their plans. Yet a divorce could have been avoided. Friends would have been peeved. The mother-of-the-bride would have been humiliated. Her dad would have been angry over all the money he had spent unnecessarily.

Everyone would have gotten over it. And a divorce would have been avoided.

Spend Time with Your Potential Spouse in Their Native Setting

In our transient society people often meet one another away from their families and relatives. Often both parties are no longer living near their childhood setting. We may be attracted to someone from another country, or another culture. Or they may have grown up across town from us and attended the same schools. Yet each family has many differences. Only when we become acquainted with another's background can we fully understand them. In a real sense, we don't marry just the man or the woman, we marry them and their family—as well as the culture that formed them.

Assess Your Expectations of Marriage and of Your Intended Spouse

One of the best exercises we can make before choosing a mate is to take time to analyze our expectations: both of marriage and of our future spouse. This can be done formally, with a pastor or counselor, or simply by making a list and prioritizing it.

We do this in other areas of life. Whether it's choosing a college to attend, or deciding upon a career. We name what we want, we prioritize. We check to see what matches our list and make our decision.

Jean was widowed after her children were grown. Jean's husband had left her financially comfortable. She told me that she didn't want to fear that someone was marrying her for her money. So Jean asked God to give her a second husband who was himself financially comfortable. God honored her prayer. Jean has never had to fear that her new husband married her for her money. They've used their combined wealth to further God's work.

Keeping It Fresh

Sometimes our expectations are unreal. We may have grown up in a home that seemed ideal. We had no idea how hard our parents had worked to keep their marriage together. If so, we may expect a sort of utopia. On the other hand, we may have seen only dysfunction in the marriages of our parents and others. Hopefully this book has provided some realistic expectations of marriage—of the husband's role and the wife's role.

We can become consciously aware of what we expect in marriage, we can know what we want in our spouse. We can go to God with our list and ask if He wants us to make any adjustments in it. Then we can leave it up to Him to bring us the right partner.

Character

One of the things to look for in a potential spouse is godly character. We can start by listing their character qualities, then divide them into three groups: he/she *has*; he/she *doesn't have*; *I don't know*. This can be followed up by listing potential problems in the future for those on the Doesn't Have List. Further inquiry can be made to discover the truth about the Don't Know List. Some might want to do the same analysis of themselves.[4]

Neil Warren offers seven warnings about marriage partner choices. He calls them The Seven Deadly Mate Selection Errors:[5]

- Marrying too quickly.
- Marrying too young.

---

[4] For a list of 95 character qualities, see: *Developing Godly Character in Children*, by Beverly Caruso, Ken Marks and Debbie Peterson, Hands to Help Publishing, 2004. Find is at: www.PeteandBevCaruso.com

[5] *Finding the Love of Your Life*, Neil Warren, Focus On the Family Publishing, 1992.

- Being too eager to get married and maybe letting someone else who is overly eager push you into marriage.
- Trying to please someone else with your choice.
- Marrying before you know your potential mate in a lot of different ways.
- Marrying with unrealistic expectations.
- Marrying anyone who has a personality or behavioral problem that you're not willing to live with forever, for these problems don't vanish, and often only get worse.

How Can You Be Sure You're Not Making a Mistake?

Besides praying about and for your future spouse, we have some suggestions for this, the most important decision you'll make besides the one concerning your eternal destiny.

Seek Godly Counsel

Your parents probably know you better than you realize. They probably know what kind of spouse would meet your needs. No, we're not recommending arranged marriages. But we firmly believe that God's way is to have a level of trust and confidence between generations. In addition to our parents, this means we leave room for, and actively seek, input from those who know us best. This likely will include a pastor or a spiritual leader who has our best interests at heart.

Pete was leaving for a month-long mission trip to India. Our daughter had been seeing a young man for several months. Before Pete left he said, "If I shouldn't make it home, it's ok for Debbie to marry Dean." Of course I chided him for bringing up the possibility of something bad happening to him.

I had a deep, settled peace in my spirit as I watched those two young people fall in love during Pete's absence.

Pete was only home a few hours when Dean asked him for Debbie's hand. Pete gave him a tough time, asking fatherly questions before consenting. I watched the process in amusement knowing full well that God had already settled the matter in Pete's heart a month earlier.

It was similar to what we had experienced some twenty years earlier. After I accepted Pete's proposal, we went together to tell my mother. Her response had been, "I've been expecting this for quite a while now."

We can be confident of God's leading when parents have been praying for their children's future mate, and when the couple has been seeking God's guidance.

Are Both Under Spiritual Authority?

We can take the time to seek the counsel and blessing of those who oversee our spiritual growth. That one who holds spiritual authority must recognize that he, too, is accountable. First, to God. *"Be shepherds of God's flock that is under your care, serving as overseers—not because you must, but because you are willing, as God wants you to be...."*[6]

We need not fear to seek counsel of spiritual leaders. The leader who is leading God's way knows not only that others are given into his care, but he sees himself as their *chief servant*. In his heart is the desire to be able to empower them to be what God intends them to be, not that they should make him great, or wealthy, or powerful.[7]

---

[6] 1 Peter 5:2
[7] *Loving Confrontation*, by Beverly Caruso, Bethany House Publishers, 1988.

During our thirty-five years of pastoring we've *tied the knot* for a lot of couples. Before agreeing to officiate at the wedding we require at least one premarital counseling session. We usually identify some things that the couple needs to work on together before the wedding. Most couples are open to this. Some are offended. Some have broken their engagement upon realizing they are not compatible. There were three determined couples we knew should not marry. Pete was open with them and pointed out his concerns.

One of those couples spent nearly thirty years of marital turmoil and strife. I said of them several times, "If they can make it, anyone can." I'm happy to say that they are still married to one another today—44 years later. However, the hours of counseling, the number of fights, and the threatened suicide seem a big price to pay to get through those first thirty years.

Another of those couples seemed like the most unlikely candidates for a good marriage. We spent untolled hours with them, individually and as couples. They raised a family, stuck it out. Today there is relative peace in their home. In their case it was the children who paid the price. Each of them is still working on healing the wounds their parents' tumultuous marriage left on them.

As we expected, the marriage of the third couple didn't last one year.

Get to Know Him or Her in a Variety of Settings
Far too many couples know each other only under limited similar circumstances. On a date, at work, at church, or a few other settings. Only after we've seen a person at their best; at their worst; at ease; under stress; handing a crises; interacting with family members; when

they don't know we're around; and a host of other situations, do we begin to truly know them.

Be Not Unequally Yoked Together

You probably wouldn't have read this far in this book if you are not a believer. Yet too many Christians fail to heed the clear instruction of the Lord: *"Do not be yoked together with unbelievers. For what do righteousness and wickedness have in common? Or what fellowship can light have with darkness?*[8] Few believers will disagree with this passage in theory. Only when they allow themselves to become emotionally entangled with an unbeliever do they make excuses to disregard it.

Perhaps this is the most important thing to consider. Are both on the same spiritual track? Several sub-questions come to mind: Do both parties enjoy the same type of worship service? Some of the loneliest people in church are those whose spouse is attending another church. Do both enjoy living out their Christian faith in similar ways—such as in evangelism or by serving through deeds? If one is called to the mission field and the other has no interest in missions, someone is going to be unhappy.

Some issues to consider:

- Are we compatible in faith and life?
- Are we in agreement on major doctrines?
- Are we both actively involved in God's work?
- Is the man ready for leadership?
- Is the woman ready to be a helpmeet?
- Do we both have a regular prayer/quiet time?
- Do we both desire children? If so, how will we handle, or not handle, birth control?
- Are we in agreement on child rearing?

[8] 2 Corinthians 6:14

- Are we in agreement on financial priorities?

Is There Full Parental Consent?

This may seem strange in today's world. Yet problems with in-laws continues to be a major area of conflict in many marriages. A couple is wise who gets to know one another's family and gains the blessing of both sets of parents. If either one cannot accept and love both sets of parents, the couple should step back and deal with the unresolved issues—before the engagement.

Perhaps you've been living away from home for some time and wonder if parental approval is necessary. Receiving the blessings of one's parents establishes a wonderful foundation for a marriage to be built upon. It's worth every effort to wait until such relationships can be established rather than having to mend hurts later.

Am I Ready for Marriage?

Perhaps you haven't begun looking for a marriage partner, but are wondering if you are ready to do so. Young people are usually so occupied with finding a mate, they seldom think of preparing themselves for marriage. Some things to consider first:

- Am I spiritually mature?
- Do I have clarity of my life's purpose?
- Have I learned essential life-skills?
- Am I financially stable?
- Am I out of debt?
- Do I have marketable skills?
- Do I have extravagant items I should sell?
- Do I know how to negotiate a best buy?
- Have I experienced receiving funds in answer to prayer?
- Do I give generously?

- What is my record for paying past debts?
- Do I make decisions based on reality?
- Have I been involved in pornography or fantasy? If so, have I dealt with it and does my spouse know so he/she can help me keep free of it?
- Have I cleared previous relationships and their consequences?
- Do I have unhealthy friendships that need to be broken?
- What am I prepared to give to a marriage?

Helpful Marriage Similarities

Dr. Neil Clark Warren in his book, "*Finding the Love of Your Life.*"[9] writes, "The more a dating couple has in common, the better their chances are of developing a happy marriage. Dr. Warren claim's that a couple should share close to 40 of the elements in order to have a happy marriage. He adds that, "Every similarity is an asset."

Dimensions for Marital Compatibility[10]

Dr. Clark, the founder of eharmony.com, names *Twenty-Nine Dimensions* a couple should look for to find marital compatibility. A couple contemplating marriage could use this list by discussing each dimension and revealing their thoughts about it.

Character & Constitution:
- Good character
- Dominance vs. submissiveness
- Curiosity
- Industry
- Vitality & security

---

[9] From the web site: eharmony.com, by Dr. Neil Clark Warren.
[10] Ibid.

- Intellect
- Appearance
- Sexual passion
- Artistic passion
- Adaptability

Personality:
- Obstreperousness
- Sense of humor
- Sociability
- Energy
- Ambition

Emotional makeup & skills:
- Emotional health
- Anger management
- Quality of self conception
- Mood management
- Communication
- Conflict resolution
- Kindness
- Autonomy vs closeness

Family & values:
- Feelings about children
- Family background
- Education
- Spirituality
- Traditionalism
- Values orientation

Who Is That Walking Down the Aisle?

Keep in mind that in reality there will be three people wearing your tuxedo down the aisle of your wedding: The man you think you are

- The man she thinks your are
- The man you really are

And there will be three women wearing your wedding gown:

- The woman you think you are
- The woman he thinks you are
- The woman you really are

How blessed we are when we know we are marrying the person whom God has chosen and prepared for us.

Chapter Nineteen

Expect Your Love to Keep on Growing

We've looked at many aspects of marriage in this book. Perhaps what we've presented seems like far more work than it's worth. We can assure you it is not.

We have enjoyed more than fifty years of married life. We currently have a teenage granddaughter staying in our home. At first she made teasing remarks when she found us in our warm *good morning kiss* in the kitchen, or when she walked into a room and caught us in a smoochie hug. "Oh, you two!' or "Get a room" were her two favorites. As Monika's visit has stretched into months she's gotten used to our expressions of affection. She knows how we communicate, how we handle disagreements, and how we cover for one another by taking over the other's chores when one is tired or tied up with work or a visitor.

Monika has learned that we really are sharing a love that keeps on growing. It's something every Christian couple can enjoy as well—by applying the biblical principles we've been sharing with you.

We've enjoyed serving others as pastors, counselors, and nurturers. We've watched many couples flourish in their relationships. We've also been saddened to see a common marital weakness: many couples who love one another and enjoy being together fall into the habit of

235

letting their mutual goals and dreams become their all consuming common interests.

This is especially tempting for couples who work together in either ministry or business—though it can happen to other couples as well. They become so wrapped up in their shared project—perhaps it is buying a house and furnishing it, or raising children together—that they fail to separate their personal relationship from their partner-relationship. When they either leave the ministry or sell the business, or the children are grown many of these couples discover they have little to talk about and little else in common.

If we keep refreshing our marriage with expressions of love and respect for one another; if we recognize each others' differences and strengths; if we keep the lines of communication open and strong; if we consciously work toward meeting the others' needs; if we protect one another from the attacks of our spiritual enemy; and if we frequently have fun together—we can expect our *love to keep on growing*.

Let's close with a heart-warming report taken from the Associated Press. Our sincere prayer is that each of our readers will enjoy a love that keeps on growing—perhaps even for seventy-seven years.

The headline of this Valentine's Day story read:

Couple Married 77 Years are Committed Because They Have "Reverence" for Marriage.

Fred and Gwen Landis of Salem, Oregon celebrated their 77th wedding anniversary last October, which makes their marriage just shy of a Guinness World record of 78 years, 296 days.

Fred, 102, and Gwen, 101, have shared Valentine day rituals since they were married in 1928. But these days -- what with Fred suffering from macular degeneration and Gwen's difficulty hearing -- it will be a simple matter of leaning near each other and proclaiming firmly, "I love you."

According to the *AP* report, the Landis' met in 1924 when he was attending Albany College and she was at Simpson Bible College in Seattle. Fred reportedly attended a church where Gwen's father was the pastor, and when they were married, Gwen's father performed the ceremony. During the following 40 years, Fred pastored several small churches in the Pacific Northwest, while Gwen played the piano and organ and taught Sunday school. Together, they raised four children. In 1970, Fred retired. The couple moved to a retirement center in Salem in 1994 and today they have eight grandchildren and 19 great-grandchildren.

"They're just wonderful people. You couldn't find any better," says friend, Dorothea McAuley. "They're setting an example for everybody. They're always happy. I've never seen one of them angry. They're God's example."

The secret to their marriage? Both Fred and Gwen say it is commitment. "Sure, we've had squabbles and disagreements galore," confessed Fred. "But there's a commitment to marriage because we have a reverence to it."

Their son John, who is 67, says he continues to be amazed by his parents, their relationship and their lives. "I think - I know - they would not have lived this long singly," he said. "They keep each other going."

Reflecting on past Valentine's Days, Gwen says Fred's penchant for writing poems to her when they were courting was irresistible. Though he can

Keeping It Fresh

no longer see to write a poem, Fred's heartfelt verbal proclamation of love to Gwen this Valentine's Day is testimony of their enduring love.[1]

A Post Script:

Rev. Frederic Morrison Landis and Gwendolyn (McCrossan '25) Landis passed away on Oct. 22, 2007, and Sept. 26, 2007, respectively. The couple, *a month shy of their 79th wedding anniversary*, died within 26 days of each other. Fred was 103, and Gwen was 102. Fred and Gwen had four children, eight grandchildren, and 28 great-grandchildren.[2]

May we each enjoy a similar *Love that Keeps on Growing*.

---

[1] Associated Press Staff Writer, Teresa Neumann Reporting, February 14, 2006
[2] *The Hawk's Nest Online Community* of Simpson College, March 10, 2008

Order Info:

For additional copies of this book or information about their other works, or to schedule the Carusos for ministry | to your group:

www.PeteandBevCaruso.com

or

Caruso@across2u.com

Keeping It Fresh

About the Authors

Pete and Bev Caruso have been married for over 50 years. They have a daughter, two sons, eight grandchildren and a number of great-grandchildren, all actively serving the Lord.

The Carusos pioneered and pastored two churches for a total of thirty-five years. In those congregations they trained and sent over 100 individuals into fulltime Christian service. They have ministered in over forty nations: in villages and jails, missionary training schools and office Bible studies, open fields and conference centers.

The Carusos continue as active speakers both in the U.S. and internationally. They team-teach Marriage Enrichment Seminars. Their lively interactive presentations bring to life the principles they teach.

The Carusos live in Southern California but are available to minister wherever the Lord leads them.

www.ingramcontent.com/pod-product-compliance
Lightning Source LLC
Chambersburg PA
CBHW020442130626
46549CB00001B/270